MW01075962

40 DAYS OF

FRESH OIL
HOLY FIRE
NEW WINE

Books by Samuel Rodriguez

Persevere with Power
Power for Your Day Devotional
Your Mess, God's Miracle
Your Mess, God's Miracle Study Guide
Walk Out of Your Mess
Fresh Oil, Holy Fire, New Wine
Fresh Oil, Holy Fire, New Wine Study Guide

40 DAYS OF

FRESH OIL HOLY FIRE NEW WINE

A Devotional

SAMUEL RODRIGUEZ

Chosen

a division of Baker Publishing Group
Minneapolis, Minnesota

© 2025 by Samuel Rodriguez

Published by Chosen Books
Minneapolis, Minnesota
ChosenBooks.com

Chosen Books is a division of
Baker Publishing Group, Grand Rapids, Michigan

Printed in the United States of America

Library of Congress Cataloging-in-Publication Data
Names: Rodriguez, Samuel, author.
Title: 40 days of fresh oil, holy fire, new wine : a devotional / Samuel Rodriguez.
Description: Minneapolis, Minnesota : Chosen Books, a division of Baker Publishing Group, [2025]
Identifiers: LCCN 2024025087 | ISBN 9780800763039 (cloth) | ISBN 9781493440870 (ebook)
Subjects: LCSH: Christian life—Meditations. | Devotional literature.
Classification: LCC BV4832.3 .R635 2025 | DDC 242—dc23/eng/20240716
LC record available at https://lccn.loc.gov/2024025087

25 26 27 28 29 30 31   7 6 5 4 3 2 1

INTRODUCTION

What kind of power gets you through your day?

Everyone relies on physical power—the way your body converts food and water as fuel to produce energy so you can function. You probably draw on intellectual power as well, based on your mind's analytical abilities, your educational training, and your various life experiences. Emotional power is a necessity these days for sure, mustering your strength, character, positivity, and stability to overcome the anxiety, frustration, anger, and disappointments you encounter. Perhaps you also rely on spiritual power to get through your day, keeping your faith in God no matter what you experience, praying regularly, reading and studying the Bible, and participating in a local church body.

Despite these various kinds of power, you probably still struggle at times. You wish you had more control over your body, mind, emotions, and soul in order to grow stronger, to have more power available within you. But no matter how hard you try, your personal power remains limited.

God's power, however, is limitless.

And if you're a follower of Jesus who has accepted the free gift of salvation and welcomed God's Spirit within your heart, then His power is available to you. You're likely already aware of this fact. You know God is more powerful than everything and anyone.

Yet the power you experience in your life seems to surge. Like an electric company hit by a relentless storm, you try to keep going, but sometimes the darkness feels overwhelming. Physical challenges drain your strength and deplete your hope. Bills keep coming while income slows to a trickle. Family members disappoint you, hurt you, disrespect you. Workplaces demand more and provide less, shifting the ground beneath your feet. And the global culture today? No one can keep up with all the changes and calamities, TikToks and turmoil, politics and perils, memes and mayhem as the world spins out of control.

Which is why the only way to not only survive but thrive is to access a power source greater than your own. If you want more power in your life to do what you have not been able to do, then now is the time for a

change. It's time to experience what's already in you—
the resurrection power of Jesus!

The Word of God says, "The Spirit of God, who raised Jesus from the dead, lives in you" (Romans 8:11 NLT). This power is not simply a onetime occurrence—the Spirit is the gift that keeps on giving! Because the same Spirit that defeated death and resurrected the lifeless body of the crucified Jesus lying in the borrowed tomb sealed by a boulder is the same Spirit living in you.

This devotional collection is based on my book *Fresh Oil, Holy Fire, New Wine* and is designed to draw you closer to the Holy Spirit as you experience the same spiritual power that raised Christ from the dead in your own life. Each day's entry includes:

Your Power Principle—a key principle or lesson of truth you can apply to your own life based on what the Bible reveals about the Holy Spirit within you.

Your Power Perspective—an exploration of the key principle based on my study of God's Word and my message in *Fresh Oil, Holy Fire, New Wine*.

Your Power Portal—a thematically related and curated Scripture verse or brief passage from God's Word to empower you with the clarity of spiritual truth.

Your Power Prayer—a few sentences to lead you into greater awareness of the Holy Spirit's presence within you as you share your heart in prayer with God.

While each of the forty days builds on the others, the goal is for you to grow closer to God through your relationship with His Spirit within you. My prayer is that you will become more reliant on the Holy Spirit—the same Spirit whose resurrection power brought Jesus back to life—and experience a fresh-oil anointing, a holy-fire combustion, and a new-wine blessing.

Are you ready to experience more power in your life than ever before? To overcome every obstacle in your way—cancer, debt, depression, anxiety, addiction, bankruptcy, betrayal, unemployment? Whatever it is, the resurrection power of God's Spirit in you is more powerful!

God wants you to experience His power in ways that will open the eyes of your heart to all that is available within you. Even as you read these words, He is at work, about to explode with spiritual dynamite in every area of your life. If you are tired of not having enough power, if you are frustrated with the way your own power seems to ebb and flow, then it's time to rely fully on the power of the Holy Spirit! Now is the time to be anointed with fresh oil, to be ignited by holy fire, and to taste the joy of new wine!

—Samuel Rodriguez

Day 1

Jesus sent His Spirit to dwell in us to ignite God's power in our lives.

Receiving the gift of the Holy Spirit changes everything!

If you want to start a fire, you need three basic elements: fuel, heat, and oxygen.

Depending on the kind of fire ignited, these three components may take different forms, but all three are fundamentally necessary for combustion. For example, to start a campfire, you might gather twigs, sticks, and dry wood for fuel, use a match or lighter as a direct heat source, and rely on the great outdoors to ensure adequate oxygen. While a campfire is intentional and contained, left unattended or unextinguished, it could accidentally escalate into a deadly wildfire. The three basic elements remain the same—only on a greater scale.

To start a sustainable fire, fuel and oxygen are not enough. You need a source of heat, a power source to provide the spark of igniting the tinder. To start a spiritual fire within us, we also need a sustainable source of heat. Which is why Jesus sent His Spirit to dwell in us—to ignite God's power within us and sustain it in all areas of our lives.

No wonder, then, that the gift of the Holy Spirit appeared incendiary when it first descended upon believers. "Then, what looked like flames or tongues of fire appeared and settled on each of them. And everyone present was filled with the Holy Spirit" (Acts 2:3–4 NLT). While the timing and appearance of the Spirit's arrival may have surprised these recipients, they knew they were about to experience something special.

Jesus had prepared His followers for this gift prior to His death and resurrection. "And I will ask the Father, and he will give you another advocate to help you and be with you forever—the Spirit of truth" (John 14:16–17). After His resurrection, He once again promised them this gift and commanded them not to leave Jerusalem until they received it (Acts 1:4).

Despite anticipating and receiving the Spirit's indwelling presence at Pentecost, these early believers then had to learn to rely on His power. They had to live out the answer to Paul's rhetorical question in his letter to the Christians at Corinth: "Don't you know that you yourselves are God's temple and that God's Spirit dwells in your midst?" (1 Corinthians 3:16).

If you have invited God's Spirit to dwell in you and have chosen to follow Jesus, then you, too, must answer this question for yourself. Because knowing you have God's Spirit in you is not the same as relying on His power to become all you are meant to be. It's time to live in the fullness of God's power through the Holy Spirit within you.

SCRIPTURE

But you will receive power when the Holy Spirit comes upon you. And you will be my witnesses, telling people about me everywhere—in Jerusalem, throughout Judea, in Samaria, and to the ends of the earth.

—Acts 1:8 NLT

PRAYER

Jesus, thank You for sending the gift of the Holy Spirit to live in me. Help me to surrender my heart fully so that I can experience the Spirit's power—the same power that raised You from the dead—in all areas of my life. Amen.

It's time to live
in the fullness of
GOD'S POWER
through the
HOLY SPIRIT
within you.

Day 2

If Jesus overcame death through the power of the Holy Spirit, you can overcome anything!

What you've been through has prepared you for what God is about to ignite in you.

If the Spirit of God, who raised Jesus from the dead, lives in you, then what does this mean exactly? What's the big deal about the Spirit working more than two thousand years ago in a cave-turned-tomb in Jerusalem being the same Spirit working right now at this very moment inside you? What does this have to do with more power?

Here's the big deal: If Jesus overcame, you can overcome.

The resurrection proved that if Jesus can come back to life after the violent, brutal, torturous death He experienced, then you can come out of anything.

Anything.

The same Spirit that raised Jesus from the dead—yes, that Spirit—is the same One living inside you right now. How is this possible? Well, are you born again? Are you a Christ-follower? Did you confess with your mouth and do you believe in your heart that Jesus is the Lord and Savior of your life? Do you love the Lord your God with all your heart, with all your soul, with all your strength, and with all your mind (see Luke 10:27)?

If your answer is yes to these queries, then you must understand that you do not have a counterfeit spirit, an outdated version, an old operating system, or a basic model that's less powerful. What you have in you is not a clone, not a cheap imitation, not a replica, not a Times Square forty-dollar knockoff. Not a diluted spirit, a watered-down version, a leftover to be reheated, a flickering ember from what was once a mighty fire.

No, my friend, you have the same living Spirit of God that raised Jesus inside you right now. The same unique, empowering, emancipating, elevating Spirit that resurrected Christ lives—not visits, hovers, drifts in and out—resides, occupies, dwells, and inhabits *you*.

What Spirit are we talking about? *The* same Spirit.

Which Spirit is this? The *same* Spirit.

They're the same, really? Yes, the same *Spirit*.

The same Spirit that hovered and covered the chaotic waters at the beginning of Creation lives inside you. "The earth was formless and empty, and darkness covered the deep waters. And the Spirit of God was hovering over the surface of the waters" (Genesis 1:2 NLT). Think about this scene for a moment. The Spirit hovered and covered a mess until God said, "Let there be light" (Genesis 1:3) and kept creating from there.

Isn't it amazing that we serve a God who hovers and covers us even when we are messy, raw, in-progress, unfinished, and uncertain? He hovers and covers us until we are ready to receive His Spirit and run with His word for us. Having this same Spirit prepares us for the new creation He's establishing in us, for the illumination of His light entering our lives.

SCRIPTURE

I pray that out of his glorious riches he may strengthen you with power through his Spirit in your inner being, so that Christ may dwell in your hearts through faith.

—Ephesians 3:16–17

——————— **PRAYER** ———————

Lord, I am humbled and excited to realize that the same Spirit empowering Jesus to overcome death is the same Spirit within me. Allow me to experience the fullness of Your miraculous and limitless power today, no matter what I may encounter. Strengthen me through the presence of the Holy Spirit so that I can boldly walk by faith. Amen.

Day 3

Through His death on the cross and resurrection, Jesus provided full coverage for any and all claims on you—past, present, and future. Your coverage is sealed by the gift of the Holy Spirit!

You are legally required to have auto insurance on any operable vehicle you own. In fact, it is against the law in all fifty states—along with Washington, DC, Guam, and Puerto Rico—to drive without it. If stopped by law enforcement, you are required to show proof of insurance, usually a form prepared by your policy carrier, along with your vehicle registration.

The advantage of car insurance can be tremendous. If you crash your car and you do not have insurance, you are liable for all the damages, will be fined, and in some circumstances imprisoned. But when you are covered, your coverage provider is responsible for your fender benders and collisions, for all damages and relevant liabilities. Assuming you pay your premiums, your insurance company covers your claims so you don't have to assume liability.

Spiritually speaking, in life, the same rule applies.

If you are not covered, you are personally responsible for all liabilities, all mistakes, all sins, all failures, all crashes, and you end up in the prison of your consequences. But when you have the same Spirit that raised Jesus from the dead, you have unlimited coverage!

Glory to God, because on the cross, Jesus paid your premium once and for all. On the cross, Jesus provided full coverage for any and all claims on you—past, present, and future. Your benefits are sealed by the gift of the Holy Spirit—talk about an incentive signing bonus!

Allstate, State Farm, Progressive, and all the other insurance providers have one thing in common: None of them cover you retroactively. None of them cover your past.

But when you have the same Spirit that raised Jesus from the dead covering you, He not only covers your present, He not only covers your future, but He covers your past. And your coverage will never be cancelled. Jesus promised, "I give them eternal life, and they shall

Day 4

When the same Spirit that raised Jesus from the dead dwells in you, then fresh oil brings a new anointing. Get ready because you are about to experience a fresh anointing in the Spirit!

If the same Spirit that raised Jesus from the grave dwells in you—and He does—then it's time to turn your potential into power. If you're stuck, it's time to get unstuck. If you're plodding along, it's time to pick up the pace. If you're not sure of your direction, then it's time to confirm your destination.

How can you experience the dynamic Spirit-led, Spirit-filled, Spirit-fueled life that God has for you? While we find numerous references and descriptors for God's Spirit throughout the Bible, three stand out to express your spiritual growth—fresh oil, holy fire, and new wine. These three serve as biblical symbols of the Holy Spirit's presence, power, and purpose in our lives.

Fresh oil is about your anointing.

Throughout Scripture, in both the Old and the New Testaments, anointing with oil symbolizes God's presence, power, and purpose on people and places set apart as holy and chosen. God gave Moses the specific recipe for mixing anointing oil, which included myrrh, cinnamon, and other natural ingredients added to olive oil (see Exodus 30:22–24). Anointing oil was poured lightly on the heads of high priests, kings, and other leaders to indicate their status as God's chosen representatives to His people. The same sacred blend was also sprinkled in the Tabernacle on various items, including the Ark of the Covenant, and various tables, lamps, and altars (see Exodus 30:26–29).

In the Old Testament, when people were anointed, the oil placed on the outside represented God's presence on the inside. They were anointed from the outside in. When Jesus died on the cross, rose from the dead, and sent the gift of His Holy Spirit, He flipped the script on anointing. When we are born again, we are no longer anointed from the outside in—we are anointed from the *inside out*.

Your power does not derive from an external variable. Your power emerges out of an internal constant.

Your anointing is when the Holy Spirit inside of you works through you to change the world around you. From Genesis to Revelation, we find that God anoints what He will use for His glory. To be anointed is to be separated, put aside, for God's usage. God anoints people, places, things, and even seasons.

There is a fresh anointing coming upon you.

There is a fresh anointing coming upon your household.

There is a fresh anointing coming upon the new season before you.

God has fresh oil for you, and fresh oil means a fresh anointing. Your fresh anointing means that you are about to experience the fulfillment of new promises, occupy more roles, conquer larger territories, and enjoy greater favor, while having more influence for the glory of Jesus than ever before. Fresh oil anoints you with fresh power!

—————— **SCRIPTURE** ——————

The Spirit of the Lord is on me, because he has anointed me to proclaim good news to the poor. He has sent me to proclaim freedom for the prisoners and recovery of sight to the blind, to set the oppressed free.

—Luke 4:18

PRAYER

Lord, You have anointed me for Your purposes—thank You for all that You are doing in me and through me by the power of the Holy Spirit! I will look for opportunities today to live out my anointing in this new season of fresh oil. Amen.

Your anointing
is when the

HOLY SPIRIT

inside of you works
through you to change

THE WORLD

around you.

Day 5

Moving into your fresh-oil anointing, you are about to ignite the fire power of the Holy Spirit! There is a holy fire within you that continues to refine you and to empower you for God's purposes.

As you move into your new season of fresh oil, you are ignited by holy fire.

Before the Spirit descended on believers at Pentecost in tongues of flame (see Acts 2:3–4), John the Baptist foretold that holy fire was coming. "He will baptize you with the Holy Spirit and fire" (Matthew 3:11). Simply put, holy fire is the unlimited, unquenchable power of the Holy Spirit. The fire of God is the presence of God. "God is a consuming fire" (Hebrews 12:29). This is not a new description of the Spirit's power and presence, but one we find burning throughout the Old and New Testaments.

When God first appeared to Moses in the book of Exodus, He revealed Himself as a blazing bush. "There the angel of the LORD appeared to him in flames of fire from within a bush. Moses saw that though the bush was on fire it did not burn up" (Exodus 3:2). The Lord also accompanied the Israelites out of Egypt through the desert into the Promised Land as a pillar of fire. "By day the LORD went ahead of them in a pillar of cloud to guide them on their way and by night in a pillar of fire to give them light, so that they could travel by day or night" (Exodus 13:21).

Elijah prayed, and holy fire came down (see 2 Kings 1:10).

The Hebrew boys, Hebrew captives in Babylon who refused to renounce their faith in God, experienced holy fire the moment the fourth man showed up in the furnace (see Daniel 3:8–12, 25).

Jeremiah said he couldn't stop preaching because he had what could be described as holy fire shut up in his bones (see Jeremiah 20:9).

The holy fire of God is a sanctifying fire, a purifying fire, a consuming fire that will address and remove once and for all every vestige of toxicity, every lie of the enemy, every obstacle and impediment to the fulfillment of God's purpose in your life. Unexpected vipers may strike and latch on, but they will never survive holy fire (see Acts 28:3–5).

For the believer, holy fire will not punish you—it will protect you.

You need to get ready for the pilot light burning within you to blaze into a conflagration of God's power in your life. You need to get ready for holy-fire power. You should expect God to show up in you, with you, for you, and through you like never before.

Don't be afraid of this fire, douse it with water, or grab a fire extinguisher.

It's time to welcome holy fire in your life!

SCRIPTURE

This third I will put into the fire; I will refine them like silver and test them like gold. They will call on my name and I will answer them; I will say, "They are my people," and they will say, "The LORD is our God."

—Zechariah 13:9

PRAYER

Dear God, ignite Your Spirit within me so that I may fulfill the purposes for which You are anointing me. Today I welcome Your holy fire into all areas of my life so that I may be refined and renewed to be more like Jesus. Amen.

Day 6

Your mess is the soil for God's miracle. When
Christ restores your vision, you will see His power
unleashed in your life!

When you experience fresh oil and holy fire—
your anointing and empowerment through
the same Spirit that resurrected Jesus from
the dead—you enter a season of new wine.

It's no coincidence that Jesus blessed wine on the
night before His death and instructed His disciples to
drink it in remembrance of Him. "This wine is my blood,
which will be poured out to forgive the sins of many
and begin the new agreement from God to his people"
(Matthew 26:28 ERV). When we partake of communion
today, we continue this sacred commemoration.

It's no coincidence that at Pentecost, when Spirit-
filled believers began speaking in various languages all

at once, others mistakenly assumed they were drunk with wine (Acts 2:13). But Peter wasted no time clarifying their misperception. He not only wanted to set the record straight about the cause of their speech, but he also wanted to take the opportunity with a crowd gathered to make a direct connection to the past, to Jewish prophecy that was being fulfilled before their very eyes (Acts 2:14–25).

While the believers at Pentecost were not drunk with wine but filled with the Spirit, they had nonetheless tasted the new wine of Christ's blood shed for them on the cross. Indeed, Jesus may have foreshadowed the filling of the Holy Spirit that His followers experienced after His resurrection when He said, "And no one puts new wine into old wineskins. For the old skins would burst from the pressure, spilling the wine and ruining the skins. New wine is stored in new wineskins so that both are preserved" (Matthew 9:17 NLT).

When you have Jesus, you are no longer who you were in the past—you are a new creature in Christ. When you welcome Jesus into your heart, then you need to recognize the need for change. New wine requires new wineskins. When you are filled with the Holy Spirit, you cannot expect to act as you once did.

You cannot expect to relate as you once did.

You cannot expect to love as you once did.

You cannot expect to work as you once did.
You cannot expect to play as you once did.
You cannot expect to worship as you once did.
You cannot expect to praise as you once did.

Abiding in the same Spirit that raised Jesus from the dead means a fresh start, a clean slate. You are a new creature in Christ who has been washed white as snow by the blood of the Lamb! You have a new life in the power and freedom of God's Spirit. Your life will never be the same!

SCRIPTURE

Therefore, if anyone is in Christ, the new creation has come: The old has gone, the new is here!

—2 Corinthians 5:17

PRAYER

Lord, thank You for the new wine of grace, mercy, and transformation in my life. May Your Spirit remind me throughout today that I am Your new creation and that I cannot expect to live in the old ways. Amen.

Day 7

You are in a unique position to be both connected to God's power and filled by it. Living in the power of His Spirit, there is holy dynamite within you!

What comes to mind when you think of dynamite?

You might immediately think of a cartoon image, a lit-fuse red cylinder like the kind Wile E. Coyote used unsuccessfully against the Road Runner. Or perhaps an iconic, quirky comedy movie pops in your mind, *Napoleon Dynamite*, the 2004 independent film about an awkward young man's coming-of-age experiences. If you're more interested in history and science than pop culture, then you probably thought of Alfred Nobel, the famous namesake of the prestigious Nobel Prizes and the inventor of dynamite.

But there's one more kind of dynamite you need to know and understand—the kind that's inside of you, *holy dynamite!* Long before Nobel coined the name *dynamite* for his explosive invention, the apostle Paul lit a fuse on our understanding of spiritual power by using the same root word, *dunamis*, to describe the power available to us through the Holy Spirit (Ephesians 1:18–20).

Dunamis power explodes with miraculous and unlimited force. This is the vested and inherent power of God in us through the indwelling of the Holy Spirit—the same Spirit that exploded with life to resurrect the dead body of Jesus in the tomb. *Dunamis* is positional power, based on inherent proximity and location. Because of who you are in Christ, and because Christ is in you, you have unimaginable, indescribable, unfathomable heavenly power—in other words, holy dynamite!

While the same Spirit is our source for *dunamis* power, God's Word tells us that this kind of power can also be found in the essence of the Gospel message of salvation through Jesus: "The message of the cross is foolishness to those who are perishing, but to us who are being saved it is the power of God" (1 Corinthians 1:18). Basically, you have the dynamic power of the Gospel message within you as well!

Filled with *dunamis* power—holy dynamite—you are an overcomer, a death-defying divine conduit of unlimited spiritual power. Relying on the Holy Spirit, you have the power to step into your home and make it a place that serves the Lord. You have the power to step into your workplace and be salt and light. You have the power to step into your community, town, or city and claim it for God's Kingdom.

Because you are filled with the Spirit, you are no longer bound by your weaknesses, mistakes, struggles, and challenges—you have the power of holy dynamite to overcome them all! You can do all things through Christ who strengthens you (see Philippians 4:13). How does He strengthen you? Through His power!

SCRIPTURE

I pray that the eyes of your heart may be enlightened in order that you may know the hope to which he has called you, the riches of his glorious inheritance in his holy people, and his incomparably great power for us who believe. That power is the same as the mighty strength he exerted when he raised Christ from the dead and seated him at his right hand in the heavenly realms.

—Ephesians 1:18–20

PRAYER

God, You are even more powerful than dynamite—almighty and all-powerful! Thank You for the bold, limitless power of Your Spirit living within me. I know that Your holy dynamite can blast through any obstacle I encounter today! Amen.

Because you are filled
with the Spirit, you are

NO LONGER BOUND

by your weaknesses,
mistakes, struggles,
and challenges—
you have the power of

HOLY DYNAMITE

to overcome them all!

Day 8

Relying on the Holy Spirit, you discover rivers of living water flowing from your innermost being. Like a mighty flood, the power of the Holy Spirit is about to burst out from within you!

While *dunamis* power seems similar to holy fire, Jesus actually compared it to what we might call holy water: "Believe in me so that rivers of living water will burst out from within you, flowing from your innermost being, just like the Scripture says!" (John 7:38 TPT). Just to make it clear, John added, "Jesus was prophesying about the Holy Spirit that believers were being prepared to receive" (John 7:39 TPT).

You'll recall that Jesus had offered this living water to the Samaritan woman at the well (see John 4). And since they were there at the place where drinking water was drawn, we might have assumed that this living water was like a cool, refreshing gulp on a hot, dusty day. And most likely there's nothing wrong or inaccurate about making this assumption.

But the way Jesus described living water in reference to the Holy Spirit was not drawn from a well, poured from a bucket, or sipped from a cup. No, He said, "Believe in Me." Notice the consequence of placing your faith in Jesus Christ, the Son of God: "Rivers of living water will burst out from within you, flowing from your innermost being."

This wellspring within you flows in rivers that will burst out. We're not talking about a drinking fountain, garden hose, or fire hydrant.

We're talking about the mighty Mississippi flooding its banks.

We're talking about the Colorado River bursting through the Hoover Dam.

We're talking about rivers—notice the plural—bursting out from within you.

Not trickling or dripping—rivers of living water bursting out!

This kind of power cannot be adequately described by comparing it to water as we know it. Even as Jesus compares the Holy Spirit to this limitless geyser of living water within you, the focus is on the power. The kind of power that descended upon Jesus in the Jordan on the day He was baptized (Matthew 3:16). The kind of power that can move mountains (see Matthew 17:20) or speak into the storm, declaring, "Quiet! Be still!" (Mark 4:39).

This is the kind of power to speak life into friends and followers, commanding Lazarus to come forth, Zacchaeus to come down, and the Samaritan woman at the well to go and sin no more. This is the kind of power to cast out devils and demons, knowing full well that you are protected from harm. "I have given you authority to trample on snakes and scorpions and to overcome all the power of the enemy; nothing will harm you" (Luke 10:19).

This is the kind of power to confront every work of the enemy in front of you attempting to stop the fulfillment of your God-ordained purpose. The kind of power to say, "Get behind me, Satan! You are a stumbling block to me" (Matthew 16:23).

This is the kind of power that is divine dynamite!

SCRIPTURE

For I will pour water on him who is thirsty, and floods on the dry ground; I will pour My Spirit on your descendants, and My blessing on your offspring.

—Isaiah 44:3 NKJV

PRAYER

Jesus, You have quenched my soul's thirst with Your living water—and through the power of Your Spirit dwelling in me, I have the power of Your rivers of living water as well! Today I will offer living water to those I meet and shower them with blessings. Amen.

Day 9

If your power seems to come and go, then it's time
to reconnect to your primary Source.

Living in the holy-dynamite power of the Holy
Spirit, you can move mountains!

If you've been experiencing a power shortage in your life, then it's time to reignite your wick from the holy fire within you. If you're struggling and desperately afraid you don't have what it takes to keep going, then you need a power surge. If you're feeling trapped by over-whelming circumstances that seem beyond your control, then you need to plug in to your power source and let His holy dynamite make a way where you cannot see one.

Your power is limited—the power of the Holy Spirit exceeds anything you can imagine. God's power parted the Red Sea.

God's power defeated Goliath.

God's power led Ruth to Boaz.

God's power saved Rahab.

God's power brought down the walls of Jericho.

God's power protected Daniel in the lions' den.

God's power turned water into wine.

God's power healed lepers.

God's power turned loaves and fishes into Filet-O-Fish for five thousand.

God's power brought Lazarus back to life.

God's power loves to do the impossible!

And with God, nothing is impossible.

Too often when we feel as if we're stuck, like we're waiting on God, the truth is that He is waiting on us! He is waiting on us to rely fully on His power—not our own—and to walk by faith and not by sight.

Perhaps we sometimes struggle because we allow our connection to our power source to fray, to unravel, or to get bent out of shape. Rather than seeking a fresh filling of the Spirit, we resort to our own abilities, our own limited human power, and then wonder why we can't keep going, can't blast through, can't see God's miracle being birthed in our mess. In those moments, we must recall that Jesus said we can move mountains with even a tiny mustard grain–sized faith (Matthew 17:20). Perhaps sometimes we struggle because we settle for too little instead of believing for too much.

If your power seems to come and go, to surge sometimes and fade at other times, then it's time to reconnect.

To recharge in the fullness of the Spirit so that you can move mountains—or what might feel like a mountain in your life right now. A mountain of overwhelming debt. A mountain of recovery from addiction. A mountain of physical therapy after a serious injury. A mountain of honesty and communication after a relationship betrayal.

Holy dynamite blasts through those mountains!

Holy dynamite makes a way where you don't see one.

Holy dynamite is in you!

SCRIPTURE

Truly I tell you, if you have faith as small as a mustard seed, you can say to this mountain, "Move from here to there," and it will move. Nothing will be impossible for you.

—Matthew 17:20

PRAYER

Dear Lord, help me to trust You more as I continue to walk by faith and not by sight. Remind me to stop striving in my own efforts and to rely on the power of Your Spirit in me. Amen.

Day 10

When Jesus rose from the dead through the power of the Holy Spirit, God revealed the kind of power entrusted to you. Resurrection power exceeds any kind of power found on earth!

Filled with the holy-dynamite power of the Spirit, you are moving into your fresh anointing. You are not where you used to be, because you are not who you used to be. The old season cannot handle the new you. The old atmosphere cannot handle the new you. The old drama cannot handle the new you. You may have been born for the past season. But you are born again for the new season!

You have died to sin, and now you are a new creature in Christ! The same Spirit that raised Jesus from the dead—guess what?—*lives in you* (Romans 8:11). Not just visits. Not just drops in temporarily until the job is done or the miracle is performed. No, the same Spirit lives in you, and in Him you live and move and have your being (Acts 17:28).

If Jesus came out of the tomb, you can come out of anything. You can come out of that next storm. That next round of chemo. That next recovery group meeting. That next unexpected expense. That next cutting comment from a loved one. That next stumble when you slip. If Jesus came out of the tomb, you can come out of anything.

Jesus said, "You will receive *power*!" His power defines you. Spirit-filled people explode with the holy dynamite of God's *dunamis* power.

Holy Spirit people are not weird.

Holy Spirit people are not weak.

Holy Spirit people are not victims.

Holy Spirit people are not whiners.

Holy Spirit people are not beggars.

Holy Spirit people are powerful!

As a matter of fact, the most powerful people on the planet are not those with fame, fortune, or followers. The most powerful people on planet Earth are those filled with the Holy Spirit; therefore, let's set the record straight.

Holy Spirit people are wired, not weird.

Holy Spirit people believe and do not beg.

Holy Spirit people are known for their anointing, not for disappointing.

Holy Spirit people have power.

Holy Spirit people have *the* power!

Why? Because the Holy Spirit is the greatest empowering force in the universe! His power is unlike any other power and is over every other power. It's the kind of power that cannot be searched or found on Google, the kind that Amazon Prime does not deliver, that no government stimulus can provide, and that the CDC cannot prescribe.

This kind of power is *resurrection power*. The same—not similar to or almost like or resembling or next-best-thing—Spirit that raised Jesus Christ out of that tomb lives inside you. Everything you do, you do with divine power!

SCRIPTURE

For the Spirit God gave us does not make us timid, but gives us power, love and self-discipline.

—2 Timothy 1:7

—————————— **PRAYER** ——————————

Lord, I know I tend to rely on my own power without even realizing it at times. Today, allow the Spirit to prompt me when I try to run ahead or trail behind You instead of living by faith and relying on Your resurrection power. Amen.

Filled with
the holy-dynamite

POWER

of the Spirit,
you are moving into your

FRESH ANOINTING.

Day 11

Your life is an advertisement for God's life-changing, heart-transforming, body-healing, mind-calming power! Others see the power of the Holy Spirit in everything about you.

Marketing, promoting, and advertising permeate our world today. The days of billboards and TV commercials have become moments of pop-up ads and social media influencers. Parks and sports facilities are named for their corporate sponsors. Movie trailers and online teasers create viewer anticipation. Product giveaways and free trials get consumers hooked so they will pay for those items and services.

Whether you realize it or not, you are also a living advertisement—your life is a trailer for God's truth! You will recall Paul's prayer for the believers in Ephesus: "I pray that you will continually experience the immeasurable greatness of God's power made available to you through faith. Then your lives will be an advertisement of this immense power as it works through you!" (Ephesians 1:19 TPT). Relying on the Holy Spirit, you exude God's power!

As God's immense power works through us, our lives become living advertisements of His dynamic, explosive, unlimited *dunamis* power at work. When holy dynamite ignites within us, others notice! How could they not see a difference in our lives? They can tell we are not who we used to be. We are not doing things the way we used to do them.

And what makes the difference? The same Spirit who raised Jesus from the dead dwells inside you. The same Spirit who made you lives inside you. The architect is now the tenant. What is the Holy Spirit's permanent address? *You!*

God's Word confirms His residence within you: "The Spirit of God has made me; the breath of the Almighty gives me life" (Job 33:4). Paul asked, "Don't you know that you yourselves are God's temple and that God's Spirit dwells in your midst?" (1 Corinthians 3:16). We are Holy Spirit–led people of the head, heart, and hand, with heads full of conviction informed by the Spirit, hearts full of compassion inspired by the

Spirit, and hands full of charitable acts imparted by the Spirit—we know it, we feel it, we live it. And we also show it!

Where can someone find the Spirit? Wherever they find you! Where can your friends, family, frenemies, and followers find Him when they are in need? Wherever they find you! You are a living, breathing, walking, and talking advertisement for the Spirit in you.

In your words.

In your look.

In your posts.

In your actions.

In your attitude.

In your touch.

In your values.

In your prayers and in your praise.

You are advertising the same Spirit that raised Jesus from the dead!

SCRIPTURE

Sing to the LORD, praise his name; proclaim his salvation day after day. Declare his glory among the nations, his marvelous deeds among all peoples.

—Psalm 96:2–3

PRAYER

Dear God, I want others to know You and to experience Your mercy and goodness just as I have. Let my life be an advertisement of Your love, Your truth, and Your power. Today, I want others to see Your Spirit through what I say and what I do. Amen.

Day 12

The Holy Spirit is freedom, and the same Spirit is in you. When you're born again, freedom is your spiritual birthright!

Others see in you what you experience in the power of God's Spirit. With God's *dunamis* power inside you, you cannot be powerless—it's impossible. Once anointed with fresh oil, Holy Spirit people are the most powerful people on the planet—because the same Spirit that raised Jesus from death to life is the Source of their power. If the Holy Spirit brought your Savior out of the tomb, He can bring you out of anything!

When you're in a tomb, the Spirit has a plan to bring you back to life. When you're in a prison, the Spirit has the power to unlock your cell. When you're in a corner, the Spirit makes a way where there was a wall.

Using God's power to liberate you is another glorious blessing of the Holy Spirit within you. "Now the Lord is the Spirit, and where the Spirit of the Lord is, there is freedom" (2 Corinthians 3:17 ESV). This is eternal, biblical truth about God's precious Spirit—both who He is and what He does. Where the Holy Spirit is Lord, there is freedom. Where is the Holy Spirit? In you; therefore, freedom is in you as well!

What kind of freedom are we talking about? The most important, essential, vital freedom in existence—your spiritual freedom. Holy Spirit freedom!

How is your spiritual freedom distinct from other kinds of freedom? According to the *Merriam-Webster Online Dictionary*, *freedom* is defined as "the quality or state of being free, such as: the absence of necessity, coercion, or constraint in choice or action; liberation from slavery or from the power of another."[1] Other synonyms for *freedom* include *independence*, *liberty*, *autonomy*, and *being unrestricted*. The opposite of freedom is captivity, oppression, or bondage.

Just to clarify further, your freedom in the Holy Spirit does not come from ancient philosophies based on the Egyptians, the Greeks, or the Romans. The

1. *Merriam-Webster.com Dictionary*, s.v. "freedom," accessed January 29, 2024, http://www.merriam-webster.com/dictionary/freedom.

freedom that you have did not come when King John signed the Magna Carta in 1215. Your freedom did not originate with the Founding Fathers or their vision for government. Your freedom does not come from George Washington, John Adams, Thomas Jefferson, James Madison, or James Monroe.

Your freedom begins and ends with the Gospel of Jesus Christ! The sacrifice He paid on the cross secured your freedom for all eternity. Once you have been freed by Jesus, you can never be contained or constrained again. "So if the Son sets you free, you will be free indeed" (John 8:36 ESV).

Freedom is power.

Freedom and faith destroy fear.

Freedom has no bars, walls, chains, or locks.

The freedom that you have comes from the most transformative, powerful force on the planet—the Holy Spirit of God!

─────────── **SCRIPTURE** ───────────

For freedom Christ has set us free; stand firm therefore, and do not submit again to a yoke of slavery.

—Galatians 5:1 ESV

───────────── **PRAYER** ─────────────

Lord, You have liberated me from the bondage of sin and given me new life through Jesus. Thank You that the enemy cannot overcome me, because greater is He who is in me than he who is in the world. Through the power of Your Spirit in me, I am an overcomer! Amen.

If the Holy Spirit
brought your Savior
OUT OF THE TOMB,
He can bring you
OUT OF ANYTHING!

Day 13

The freedom you have in the Holy Spirit is the ultimate liberation from all that has been holding you
back. Let your freedom ring so that it echoes in
every area of your life!

One of our country's most patriotic treasures is
the Liberty Bell, proudly displayed in the City
of Brotherly Love, Philadelphia, Pennsylvania.
While it has that famous crack silencing its clapper, the
ideals it embodies continue to resonate.

But *our* symbol of liberty echoes with the power
of God's Spirit. Through the power of the cross, our
freedom rings loud and clear and can never be silenced.
Through the power of the Gospel, our freedom rings
true with great news.

The great news is that through Jesus Christ, you can
be free from a life of sin (Revelation 1:5).

The great news is that you now know the truth and it shall set you free (John 8:32).

The great news is that in Christ, you can be free from the torment of fear (2 Timothy 1:7).

The great news is that in Christ, you can be free from the sentence of eternal condemnation (Romans 8:1).

The great news is that when you know His freedom, your life can never be the same, because you are a new creature in Christ (2 Corinthians 5:17).

Free people live differently, look differently, and love differently.

Free people are baptized with Christ in Romans, crucified with Christ in Galatians, seated with Christ in Ephesians, strengthened by Christ in Philippians, hidden in Christ in Colossians, and reigning with Christ in Revelation. Behold the Lamb!

Free people can't be silenced.

Free people can't be trampled on.

Free people can't be placed in a corner.

Free people can't be defeated.

Free people can't go back to the old way.

If you have not been living in the fullness of your freedom, it's time to redeem the narrative. Your story is not what it used to be. Your Savior has authored new chapters more glorious than what you can imagine. No matter what you thought you were or would always be, your script has been flipped. You are free to be who God created you to be!

No longer will you settle for the illusion of freedom. People on probation with an ankle bracelet may look free, act free, and dress free, but the moment they cross a certain line, they will soon discover their freedom is an illusion. They are still bound to the consequences of what they've done. They are still limited in their mobility by the punishment for their crime.

God wants to set you free from the illusion of freedom. Free from the "bracelet" of religious coercion. Free from secular intimidation. Free from generational manipulation. Free from self-mutilation.

You are free forevermore in the power of the Holy Spirit!

Let your freedom ring!

——————— **SCRIPTURE** ———————

But now that you have been set free from sin and have become slaves of God, the benefit you reap leads to holiness, and the result is eternal life.

—Romans 6:22

PRAYER

Jesus, thank You for being the Source of my freedom from sin. Today I will rely on the power of the Holy Spirit—the same Spirit that raised You from the dead—to break free from all the snares and cares of the world that would entangle me. Amen.

Day 14

Your freedom in the Spirit is contagious! When others see the power of God at work in your life, they will want the same freedom in their own lives as well.

The Spirit of Jesus sets people—people just like you and me—free. Wherever the Spirit of the Lord is, there is freedom. The Spirit of the Lord is in you, and other people cannot help but notice. Holy Spirit people are free people. Free from everything that has tried to encumber them, to hold them, to bear down on them, to crush them, to overwhelm them. No more!

Your freedom is power. Your freedom sends fear running. Your freedom has no walls. Yes, Holy Spirit people are free. And free people—they free people!

The most powerful human on the planet is a person set free by the Spirit of the living God! Why? Because free people can do what others cannot.

It was a free man who approached Pharaoh in Egypt and said, "Let my people go" (Exodus 9:1).

It was a free man who stepped into the Promised Land and declared, "As for me and my household, we will serve the LORD" (Joshua 24:15).

It was a free man who stared down a giant called Goliath and said, "You come against me with sword and spear and javelin, but I come against you in the name of the LORD Almighty, the God of the armies of Israel" (1 Samuel 17:45).

It was a free group of people who refused to bow and subsequently exhibited freedom even in the midst of a fiery furnace (Daniel 3:16–22).

It was a free man who prayed down fire from heaven and then shouted, "Get ready. Here comes the rain" (see 1 Kings 18:44).

It was a free man who opened his mouth and said, "I can't stay quiet, I must prophesy. It is just like fire shut up in my bones" (see Jeremiah 20:9).

It was a free woman who said, "Your people will be my people and your God my God" (Ruth 1:16).

It was a free woman who said, "If I only touch his cloak, I will be healed" (Matthew 9:21).

Eternal freedom, freedom of the soul, freedom of the spirit, and freedom to go beyond existence to truly living does not come from leaders or governments, individuals or institutions. Our freedom comes from the One who wrote the Law with one finger and grace with both hands. Our freedom comes from the Great Liberator and Lover of our souls. Once we have been set free, we want everyone else to experience the same freedom that has liberated us.

Our freedom is contagious and frees others.

Free people free people!

SCRIPTURE

Therefore, my friends, I want you to know that through Jesus the forgiveness of sins is proclaimed to you. Through him everyone who believes is set free from every sin.

—Acts 13:38–39

PRAYER

Lord, empower me through Your Spirit to live as someone who is free indeed! Give me a spirit of boldness so that my words and actions will demonstrate spiritual freedom to those around me. Open my eyes today to opportunities to share the message of the Gospel, in both word and deed, with those I encounter. Amen.

Once we have been
SET FREE,
we want everyone else
to experience the same
FREEDOM
that has liberated us.

Day 15

When you are filled with the power of the Holy Spirit, you receive the bilingual benefit of a new language! You become fluent in the language of grace, power, and freedom.

If you have ever pursued learning a new language, you know there are plenty of educational options. Depending on your learning style and availability, you might choose in-person classroom instruction, private tutoring, online conversation partners, or immersive experiences in a community of native speakers. Or perhaps you grew up in a bilingual home or community, which facilitated your linguistic fluency organically.

Regardless of your linguistic education in the past, you have a bilingual ability you may not be using. If you have been born again in the Spirit and accepted the free gift of salvation through the sacrifice of Jesus on the cross and the power of His resurrection, then you are already fluent in the divine dialect of faith. Fresh oil anoints your capacity for divine communication. The language of the Holy Spirit makes you a native speaker of your true homeland—heaven. "For this world is not our home; we are looking forward to our everlasting home in heaven" (Hebrews 13:14 TLB).

When you are filled with the Spirit of God, the first sign you see is that you speak what you have never spoken before. This fact is based on God's Word and its record of what occurred at Pentecost following Christ's ascension: "They saw what seemed to be tongues of fire that separated and came to rest on each of them. All of them were filled with the Holy Spirit and began to speak in other tongues as the Spirit enabled them" (Acts 2:3–4).

Just like the 120 believers that day, we cannot be filled with the same Spirit that descended at Pentecost and remain silent. We are compelled by the power in us to communicate the truth of the Gospel, the truth of who God is, the truth of His Spirit's power. When you have an individualized, personalized tongue of fire from the same Spirit engulf you, your language changes!

Why would you suddenly need a new language? Why does being filled by the Spirit make you spiritually bilingual? Because we must know how to communicate the Word Made Flesh, Jesus Christ. We must allow the holy fire within us to burn through the lies and deception of the enemy.

We must speak the language of the Spirit because we know that if we want to change the culture, we must change the language. Change your language, change your world. We can change the culture if we change our language. Imagine speaking in the language of the Spirit. Imagine saying what the Holy Spirit wants to say. Imagine listening to and comprehending the voice of God.

When you are filled with the same Spirit, you speak what you have never spoken before. You receive the bilingual benefits of speaking fluently in the language of holiness, freedom, and power.

 **SCRIPTURE**

"Return home and tell how much God has done for you." So the man went away and told all over town how much Jesus had done for him.

—Luke 8:39

PRAYER

Dear Lord, today I want to speak what I have never spoken before and proclaim Your goodness and faithfulness. Allow Your message to flow through me as You provide the words in the spiritual language of freedom and power. Amen.

Day 16

You cannot be filled with the power of the Holy Spirit and remain silent! Your life, your actions, and your words proclaim the goodness of God for all to hear.

When you live in the power of the Holy Spirit, you are compelled to praise God with everything in you. Even before praise takes shape in music, even before words come together as lyrics, praise starts with a sound—just as the arrival of the Holy Spirit at Pentecost began with a blast of what must have sounded like a tornado: "Suddenly they heard the sound of a violent blast of wind rushing into the house from out of the heavenly realm. The roar of the wind was so overpowering it was all anyone could bear!" (Acts 2:2 TPT).

They heard a sound—and what a sound! It was a sound that commanded their attention suddenly, a sound that could not be ignored, a sound that announced their anointing. Because being filled by the Holy Spirit always begins with a sound.

A sound is the initial evidence that a shift is taking place. A sound is the first indicator of transformation. A sound is the immediate response to revelation. From Genesis to Revelation and throughout the pages of the Bible, the greatest shifts began with a sound. With a sound, the Architect of the universe pushed back darkness when He said, "Let there be light" (Genesis 1:3).

With a sound, Joshua began the conquest of the Promised Land as the Israelites shouted and the walls came tumbling down (see Joshua 6:20). With a sound, Gideon's army defeated the Midianite marauders by breaking the jars that covered the fire torches as they shouted, "A sword for the Lord and for Gideon!" (Judges 7:20).

With a sound, the prophet Elijah prophesied the end of the drought by declaring, "I hear the sound of abundant rain coming our way!" And sure enough, God's prophet then told Ahab, "Go, eat and drink, for there is the sound of a heavy rain" (1 Kings 18:41).

With a sound, the prophet Ezekiel saw a vision, the coming together of an army: "As I was prophesying, there was a noise, a rattling sound, and the bones came together, bone to bone" (Ezekiel 37:7).

With a sound, a blind man prompted Jesus to look his way and give him his sight by simply shouting, "Son of David, have mercy on me!" (Luke 18:38).

With a sound, Bartimaeus heard that it was Jesus of Nazareth and began to shout and say, "Jesus, Son of David, have mercy on me!" (Mark 10:47).

And guess who's coming back with a sound! "For the Lord himself will come down from heaven, with a loud command, with the voice of the archangel and with the trumpet call of God" (1 Thessalonians 4:16).

Relying on God's Spirit within you, your life makes a heavenly sound!

SCRIPTURE

Shout for joy to the LORD, all the earth, burst into jubilant song with music; make music to the LORD with the harp, with the harp and the sound of singing, with trumpets and the blast of the ram's horn—shout for joy before the LORD, the King.

—Psalm 98:4–6

—— PRAYER ——

Lord, I give You thanks and praise with every fiber of my being! No matter what challenges I'm facing, no matter what I encounter today, I can rejoice in the knowledge of Your power in me through the Holy Spirit. I can no longer remain silent about all You have done for me! Amen.

Day 17

Empowered by God's Spirit, you can fill the world with the joyful sound of the Gospel message! You can speak God's grace, love, mercy, truth, and hope into the world's discord.

At Pentecost, the Holy Spirit's arrival came with a violent blast of wind that apparently overwhelmed those receiving the gift of His indwelling presence. They may have panicked momentarily or wondered if this mighty wind would whisk them away. But then it became clear to them that this rushing roar audibly expressed the power of God in their midst.

Spiritually speaking, a sound is the beginning of a shift. The greater the sound, the greater the shift. The louder the sound, the louder the shift echoes. A holy sound will push back darkness. A righteous sound will make the walls come down. A prophetic sound will release abundant rain. A courageous sound will confuse the enemy. A worshiper's sound will make Jesus look your way. A Spirit-filled believer's sound will become praise.

This is why you cannot be silent. This is why you cannot be complacent. This is why you cannot be muted. The Church of Jesus Christ was born on Pentecost—and it was born with a sound!

There is no such thing as a church without a sound. There is no such thing as Christianity on mute. There is no such thing as a silent Christ-follower. There is no such thing as a complacent disciple of Jesus.

As people of the Spirit, if we don't hear the sound, then we must make a sound. And the sound that comes from the Spirit within us will always be louder than the sound that comes from the world around us. The Church must be louder than the culture. And louder does not mean irritating or abrasive, harsh or annoying, even if the sound of our message may grate on ears unwilling to hear truth. Louder voices bring music where there is noise, harmony where there is discord.

It's time for you to stop being so quiet and start making some noise. You can fill the world with the sound of grace, love, mercy, truth, and hope. You can fill the world with the joyful noise of the Gospel. You can fill the world with the sound of redemption, renewal, and reconciliation. You were born with a sound, so you live with the sound. You were born again with a sound, so your life in the Spirit has a sound.

Outside your walls, you can hear the sound of a broken world, the angry cries and weary sighs of a culture obsessed with cancellations, wokeness, offensiveness, unforgiveness, hypersensitivity, and victimization. You can hear the sounds of anxiety, depression, fear, consternation, angst, violence, hatred, chaos, pain, hurt, and brokenness.

But let not your heart be troubled. You are a Pentecost person. You are filled with the same Spirit. And the sound you make is praise!

--- **SCRIPTURE** ---

For we speak as messengers approved by God to be entrusted with the Good News. Our purpose is to please God, not people. He alone examines the motives of our hearts.

—1 Thessalonians 2:4 NLT

PRAYER

Dear God, give me wisdom and discernment about what to say to those who do not know You and when to say it. Let my life speak of Your presence, purpose, and power. Let my life be a joyful noise praising You! Amen.

Day 18

The sound of the Spirit in you cannot be muted! You are hearing what you have never heard before— the voice of God speaking directly to your heart.

Sound is a mechanical wave, which means that it requires substance—such as air or water—to travel through in order to vibrate and produce sound waves. In space, there is no air, no atmosphere, so sound has nothing through which to travel. If someone were to scream in space, the sound wouldn't leave their mouths.

Considering the way sound needs a source and a substance, you might wonder why the people around us don't always seem to hear the Good News about Jesus that we want to share. We have the ultimate Source, the Holy Spirit, speaking in us and through us, so why don't others listen? Why isn't the world becoming more like the Church? Why are they ignoring our sound?

Perhaps it's because they cannot hear us. What if the problem is not the sound, but the atmosphere? When we as Christians whine more than we worship, we don't create an atmosphere capable of carrying our sound—we create a vacuum. When we preach more about the problems than we do about the promises, that vacuum will not carry a holy sound.

But atmospheres shift when architects alter the environment.

God is anointing men and women from every generation, not just to shift the current cultural atmosphere, but to *create* a God-honoring, spiritual atmosphere. If you are filled with the same Spirit that ignited tongues of holy fire on the believers at Pentecost, then you are already altering your atmosphere. You may be shifting what's around you or creating a new atmosphere altogether—or both!

When your sounds come from the Spirit, you sing a new song into the spiritual silence of the world's culture. To voice this new song, you don't need extra lung power, breath control, or a strong diaphragm—you must simply rely on the power of God's Spirit! Because the sound of Pentecost is God in you.

And when the same Spirit is in you, you also hear what you haven't heard before. By faith in the name of

Jesus and through the power of the Holy Spirit, you can hear God's voice speak directly to your heart.

You can hear the sound of prophecy (Ezekiel 37:7).

You can hear the sound of restoration (Job 42:12–13).

You can hear the sound of change (Amos 9:13).

You can hear the sound of greater things (John 14:12).

You can hear the sound of the enemy being crushed (Romans 16:20).

Just like those believers at Pentecost, you can hear a wind like no other blowing change into the atmosphere around you!

SCRIPTURE

But I tell you that everyone will have to give account on the day of judgment for every empty word they have spoken. For by your words you will be acquitted, and by your words you will be condemned.

—Matthew 12:36–37

PRAYER

Jesus, help me to follow Your example in how I use my words. Empower my speech to reflect Your love, Your grace, Your peace, and Your righteousness. Open my ears today to hear the voice of Your Spirit within me so that I may speak Your truth into the clamor of the world. Amen.

Just like those
BELIEVERS
at Pentecost,
you can hear a wind
LIKE NO OTHER
blowing change
into the atmosphere
around you!

Day 19

There's a difference between feeling God's presence in your life and the filling of the Holy Spirit in you! No matter what you're facing or how you feel, you can rely on the Spirit for the power you need to persevere.

You are filled with a new sound because there's a difference between *feeling* God's presence and being *filled* with the Spirit of God. He does not only want you to feel His presence—He wants you to be filled with His Spirit (Ephesians 5:18). When you are filled, the sound you make resonates with the power of the cross and the Spirit of the empty tomb.

Jesus paid the price so that you can go beyond a visitation of the Spirit to receive habitation by the Spirit. Jesus came so that we can go from God with us to God in us. He shed His blood not just for His Spirit to move *over* us, but for His Spirit to move *in* us.

When you are filled by the same Spirit who arrived with the sound of a mighty wind, your own sound becomes a song of praise—no matter how you feel. Your praise defines and refines you. Your praise is not based on a feeling, but on a filling.

It's easy to feel like praising God and giving Him thanks and worshiping Him when you're enjoying the abundance of His blessings, when your family is healthy, when your car works, or when your bills are paid on time. When life seems to be working in your favor, your gratitude spills out in praise to the Source of all goodness. When you can see God clearly at work around you, giving thanks is not a challenge.

But it's tough to feel like praising God and worshiping Him when your life seems to be falling apart. When you're struggling hour to hour, day by day. When your body throbs with pain that no medication seems to alleviate. When your child's addiction weighs on your heart. When your car breaks down on the side of the road. When you don't have the money to pay last month's bills.

That's when you must remember: You don't praise because of a feeling, but because of a filling! When you are filled by the same Spirit who raised Jesus from the dead, you know that all things work together for your good according to God's all-knowing plans. When you are filled by the same Spirit who descended on the believers in the Upper Room, you know that you have supernatural power to endure natural disaster, personal crisis, family turmoil, and devastating loss.

Why? Because you choose to trust God even when you don't understand all that's going on around you. Because you believe His promises will be fulfilled. Because you know the same Spirit dwells in you that raised Jesus from the dead!

SCRIPTURE

Even though I walk through the darkest valley, I will fear no evil, for you are with me; your rod and your staff, they comfort me.

—Psalm 23:4

PRAYER

Lord, You are my good Shepherd and my Protector, my Provider, and my Comforter. Thank You that Your Spirit fills me with Your presence and power no matter how I'm feeling. Today I will rest in the peace of knowing I'm filled with the power of the Holy Spirit. Amen.

Day 20

Praise becomes the soundtrack of your soul when you focus on your filling and not your feeling. As you rely on the power of God's Spirit, you learn to sing a new song!

W hen you receive the same Spirit in you that raised Christ from the dead (Romans 8:11), and when you are filled with the same Spirit, praise is the soundtrack of your soul. In good times and hard times, in pain and in comfort, in joy and in sorrow, in grief and in gratitude, no matter what you're feeling, you praise from your filling.

In order to praise with a new song, you must allow God to transform your mourning into dancing, and you must recognize the old song has played out. The record player is turning, but the needle has reached the last track in the vinyl. The old song no longer applies to where you are. The old song cannot express the power and freedom you have in the Spirit of God.

You are familiar with that old playlist of broken promises and failed attempts, of hatred and racism, of intolerance and fear, and of division and strife. You've heard the old album of cultural decadence and spiritual apathy with its mind-numbing melody and languishing lyrics, the irrelevant song of hopelessness and despair.

When you are filled by the same Spirit that raised Jesus from the tomb, you cannot remain silent; you must sing a new song—and you are not alone in singing it! This new song will not be sung exclusively by a black choir or a white ensemble, by a Latino band or an Asian soloist.

This new song will be sung by a multiethnic, divinely diverse choir washed snow-white by the blood of the Lamb, Jesus Christ. This new song drowns out the fading chorus of captivity with its repulsive refrain. This new song raises the volume with prophetic power and a rhythm of revival. This new song reminds us of where we have been, where we are, and where we are going. This new song praises God for always making a way.

For every Pharaoh, there is always a Moses.

For every Goliath, there is always a David.

For every Nebuchadnezzar, there is always a Daniel.

For every Jezebel, there is always an Elijah.

For every Herod, there is always Jesus.

For every devil that rises up against us, there is always a mightier God rising up for us.

Your new song unites families in the love of Christ and the power of the Spirit.

Your new song provides a prophetic prescription to end poverty.

Your new song restores justice and brings freedom to the captives.

Your new song never ends!

SCRIPTURE

He put a new song in my mouth, a hymn of praise to our God. Many will see and fear the Lord and put their trust in him.

—Psalm 40:3

PRAYER

Dear God, I am so grateful that You have given me a new song! You have turned my mourning into dancing with praise as the playlist for my life. My heart will sing Your new song today, reminding me that You always make a way, telling others of Your goodness. Amen.

For every devil
that rises up

AGAINST US,

there is always
a mightier God

RISING UP FOR US.

Day 21

When you are filled with God's power, you wait *in* the Spirit—not *on* the Spirit! How you wait on what God has for you often prepares you for what you're waiting on.

If you have ever sat in a hospital lobby, patient's room, or ER, then you know waiting can be scary. Waiting for your child to come through surgery. For a parent to be taken off life support. For an update from the surgeon about your spouse, brother, or sister brought in by ambulance after the accident. For the medical results showing whether the chemo is working.

So much uncertainty.

So many doubts.

Waiting by faith is especially agonizing since we can't see how God is working or know what His answers to our prayers might be. Based on what we see in the Bible, though, *wait* and *suddenly* are part of the same faith continuum. Throughout Scripture, we see men and women of faith who waited: Abraham, Job, Esther, Daniel, Zechariah, Elizabeth, Mary, Samuel, Anna, the disciples, and so many others. Their wait was rewarded when it was least expected.

And *how* they waited prepared them for *what* they waited on.

They worshiped while they waited. They prayed, fasted, wept, and declared the promises of God. Their waiting literally changed the world, because people who wait in the Spirit are the people who experience a *suddenly* that arrives like a mighty, rushing wind.

Men and women filled with the Holy Spirit know that they wait *in* the Spirit—not *on* the Spirit. They know that waiting in the Spirit is not the same thing as waiting *for* God to do what we want Him to do, what we're hoping and praying He will do—because the Spirit of God is always at work—in us, through us, around us, beyond us. This is true even when we have no evidence based on logic, probability, past experiences, or our human senses.

When we find ourselves waiting for God to open a door, we need to hit *pause* on our fear and confront it with our faith. Too often, we seem to get caught up in both a Church culture and an individual mindset focused on the idea of open doors. We talk about waiting for God to open a door, waiting on His power to make a way, and waiting on His guidance to reveal how we can move forward.

None of this is wrong.

But when we limit ourselves to open doors, then we minimize the beauty and blessing of what takes place behind closed doors. We overlook what God is already doing *where we are*—to prepare us, educate us, equip us, and empower us. We miss out on the intimacy with God that takes place before the next door gets opened.

Don't lose sight of how God is preparing you for your *suddenly*!

—————— **SCRIPTURE** ——————

Who hopes for what they already have? But if we hope for what we do not yet have, we wait for it patiently.

—Romans 8:24–25

—————— **PRAYER** ——————

Lord, grant me the patience to wait on Your divine timing. Thank You that I can wait in Your Spirit, knowing that You are preparing me while I wait. Keep the eyes of my heart focused on You where I am, even when I'm eager to look ahead. Amen.

Day 22

While you are waiting in the power of the Spirit, do not overlook the peace available to you. In our times of waiting, Jesus often meets us behind a closed door!

After the resurrection, Jesus appeared to His disciples, not before an open door, but behind a closed door: "On the evening of that first day of the week, when the disciples were together, with the doors locked for fear of the Jewish leaders, Jesus came and stood among them and said, 'Peace be with you!'" (John 20:19).

The disciples were afraid—and for good reason. The Jewish authorities were spreading rumors that Jesus had not risen from the dead, but that His body had merely been stolen by His followers to stage the appearance of a resurrection. Some of them had seen the risen Lord in person, but others, particularly Thomas, weren't so sure they believed what they heard.

And then suddenly, Jesus appeared and offered them—a key to open the door? A Xanax to calm their nerves? A pep talk on courage? No, Jesus appeared and offered them *peace*.

Sometimes closed doors have much more value than open doors. Closed doors usually precede open doors. But in the meantime, we can experience the presence of Jesus and receive His peace. The supernatural, heavenly peace that surpasses human understanding. The peace that comes from waiting *in* the Spirit and not *on* the Spirit.

The disciples not only heard Jesus, they not only saw Jesus, but at least one of them touched Him. He felt His wounds and saw the piercing in His side. Spiritually speaking, before the disciples changed the world, they met with Jesus behind a closed door.

In our times of waiting, Jesus often meets us behind a closed door. Sometimes God will even close a door in order to reveal something to you that otherwise you would not see. Do not overlook the gifts on this side of a closed door.

A closed door with Jesus equals revelation.

A closed door with Jesus equals intimacy.

A closed door with Jesus equals an encounter like never before.

Behind closed doors, amazing things happen. If you are filled with the Spirit but are waiting, and if you feel as if the door has closed in front of you, don't assume you're stuck in place. Don't curse the closed door. Don't even disregard the closed door.

When you're waiting in the Spirit behind a closed door, it only means that you are about to touch Jesus and experience His peace in an unprecedented manner.

Believe by faith that your closed-door season prepares you for your open-door season. A closed-door season in which Jesus changes you often comes before the open-door season in which you change the world.

Praise God for your open doors—and thank Him for your *closed doors* as well!

SCRIPTURE

Peace I leave with you; my peace I give you. I do not give to you as the world gives. Do not let your hearts be troubled and do not be afraid.

—John 14:27

PRAYER

Dear Jesus, thank You for meeting me behind closed doors while I wait on what's next. Replace my fear with peace and my doubts with faith. Today I will rest in the power of Your peace provided through Your Spirit in me. Amen.

A closed-door
season in which
JESUS CHANGES YOU
often comes
before the open-door
season in which

**YOU CHANGE
THE WORLD.**

Day 23

No matter what door stands in your way, God always shows up for you! Don't allow your wounding to stand in the way of experiencing what Jesus has done for you.

Just because a door closes does not mean it can stop God from showing up—because a closed door cannot stop a resurrected Jesus.

Even when others close your door, Jesus still shows up.

Even when circumstances close your door, Jesus still shows up.

Even when you close the door yourself, whether intentionally or unintentionally, Jesus still shows up. No matter who you are, where you are, or what that door is made of, Jesus will always show up!

When Daniel was placed in the lions' den and they sealed it, God showed up.

When the Hebrew boys were in the fiery furnace, God showed up.

When the cold, lifeless body of Jesus was placed in a borrowed tomb, God showed up.

No matter what door stands in your way, God is showing up for you.

Behind closed doors, when you're waiting in the Spirit, you see the wounds that forgave your sins and the stripes that healed you. "Then he showed them the wounds of his hands and his side—they were overjoyed to see the Lord with their own eyes!" (John 20:20 TPT).

Jesus showed them His wounds and revealed His side, where He was pierced. Why would He do that? He revealed His wounds and pierced side to confirm His identity. He was not showing what they'd done to Him; Jesus was showing what He did for *us*! He was not just showing His wounds and stripes; He was showing the disciples their forgiveness—and your healing!

When you look at the wounds of Jesus, you see your forgiveness.

When you look at the stripes of Jesus, you see your healing.

When you experience the presence of Jesus, you are dead to sin and alive to righteousness.

By showing up behind closed doors with His disciples, Jesus makes an implicit declaration of eternal truth: "They tried everything and yet here I am. I was beaten and bloody, and yet here I am. I was parched and pierced, and yet here I am. I was mocked and denigrated, and yet here I am. And if I did it, *you* can do it."

When you find yourself in a place where the door is closed, where you feel stuck, where you assume you are waiting on God, waiting on the Spirit to move, stop and consider what the Lord has done for you. Don't let your wounding stand in your way. Don't allow your wounding to leave you waiting when you already have the same Spirit within you that raised Christ from the dead!

SCRIPTURE

But he was pierced for our transgressions, he was crushed for our iniquities; the punishment that brought us peace was on him, and by his wounds we are healed.

—Isaiah 53:5

PRAYER

Lord, I know that nothing can stop You from showing up for me. When I feel stuck in place or grow impatient behind a closed door, allow me to see what You want to show me, to learn more of Your grace, and to experience more of Your healing presence. Amen.

Day 24

Don't stop before you see who God made you to be, what He wants to do for you, and how He wants to bless you. Don't give up before you get the gift!

Have you ever attended a party or been to visit a friend when they stopped you on your way out the door? "You can't leave until you get the gift I have for you," they might say. "Don't go anywhere! I'll be right back with it." And you're left to assume that this gift is worth the wait.

Now, multiply that kind of moment beyond measure, and you have the message Jesus gave to His disciples. After visiting His disciples behind closed doors, but before He ascended into heaven, Jesus told them not to leave too soon. He had a gift for them already prepared for delivery via Pentecost Prime to an Upper Room in Jerusalem: "Don't leave Jerusalem, but wait here until you receive the gift I told you about, the gift the Father has promised. For John baptized you in water, but in a few days from now you will be baptized in the Holy Spirit!" (Acts 1:4–5 TPT).

They wanted to leave.

It would have been logical to leave.

It made sense after the crucifixion of their Master to get out of Jerusalem before the authorities came looking for them. They probably wondered, "Are we next to be arrested falsely and killed?"

Well aware of their fear, Jesus nonetheless urged, "Don't leave yet! My present for you is more than worth the wait." He wanted His followers to trust Him, to realize that He would not ask them to hang around and wait on this amazing gift without ensuring they would be able to receive it.

The same is true for you. Jesus has already dealt with everything that has the ability to stop you, hinder you, obstruct you, impede you, or block you from experiencing the fulfillment of His promise. Jesus took care of everything that could hold back the door that now needs to be opened. Jesus took care of everything that tries to prevent you from resting in His confidence and peace.

So don't leave now! Do not stop waiting right before your *suddenly* moment. Jesus is right there with you. His Spirit is within you. Don't decide to go before you see what God wants to do for you, what He wants to give you, how He wants to bless you.

If you're tired of waiting, take heart.

If you're afraid of what happens next, fear not.

If you're disappointed by a closed door, just wait.

Do not leave Jerusalem, because the gift is worth the wait.

If you leave town now, you won't get it.

God's gift is always worth the wait!

SCRIPTURE

Be still before the Lord and wait patiently for him; fret not yourself over the one who prospers in his way, over the man who carries out evil devices! Refrain from anger, and forsake wrath! Fret not yourself; it tends only to evil. For the evildoers shall be cut off, but those who wait for the Lord shall inherit the land.

—Psalm 37:7–9 ESV

PRAYER

Heavenly Father, thank You for the many good gifts You have given me in my life. Looking back, I see how

You always keep Your promises and how You delight in blessing me with their fulfillment. I can wait with confidence today, trusting in the power of Your Spirit in me. Amen.

Do not stop waiting
right before your
SUDDENLY MOMENT.
God's gift is
ALWAYS
worth the wait!

Day 25

God is a God who saves—that's who He is! Your salvation is secure through the sacrifice of Jesus on the cross and by the power of the Holy Spirit within you.

Even before God sent His Son to die on the cross for our salvation, saving His people has always been who He is and what He's all about. God has always been a Savior and a saving God. He saved Joseph from dying as a result of his brothers' betrayal. God saved the Hebrews from permanent Egyptian captivity. The Lord saved Elijah from Jezebel, Daniel from the lions, and the Hebrew boys from a fiery furnace. God saves.

Yet every human being requires salvation way beyond circumstances, enemies, and external threats. This is why God sent His beloved Son to live, die, and defeat death once and for all, saving us from our sins and securing for us the power of His Spirit within us. This is the choice we make when we accept the free gift of grace that provides deliverance from sin and its consequences and choose to walk by faith.

Simply put, we have received what Isaiah foretold God's people: "Then your salvation will come like the dawn" (Isaiah 58:8 NLT). This is not simply a poetic simile or a great statement to pair with an Instagram image of a pink and yellow sunrise. Once God created the heavens and earth, He set the planets in motion around the sun in our solar system, resulting in night and day based on earth's rotational orbit. For us on earth, we see the sun rise every morning and the sun set every night. Since Creation, this natural trajectory perpetuates the continuity of linear time for humanity.

The rising of the sun is inevitable as long as the Lord permits it. For every person who has lived thus far in the history of our world, the rising of the sun has remained a constant, a predictable certainty. So when Isaiah says that "your salvation will come like the dawn," he means that it is certain, reliable, and already established.

Salvation is fundamental to your faith.

Salvation is foundational to your identity in Christ.

Salvation is the fulfillment of God's promise to send His Spirit.

Everyone needs to be saved. Everyone requires salvation. Because without salvation, you will not have eternal life.

No matter how good you are, what social justice cause you fight for, how much money you give to the poor, whom you know, or which church you attend, you still need to be saved. It doesn't matter how many seminary degrees, PhDs, or MDs you have framed on your walls. It's irrelevant whether you volunteer at the homeless shelter, stock the food pantry, teach the Sunday school class, or lead the small-group Bible study.

Without salvation, nothing else matters.

With salvation, you have the gift of God's Spirit in you.

SCRIPTURE

Surely God is my salvation; I will trust and not be afraid. The LORD, the LORD himself, is my strength and my defense; he has become my salvation.

—Isaiah 12:2

PRAYER

Dear God, there is nothing I can do to earn my salvation—only by Your grace and mercy can I accept it as a free gift. Thank You for being a God who saves! I am so grateful for this gift of salvation, made possible through Your Son, Jesus, and by the power of Your Holy Spirit within me. Amen.

Day 26

Your salvation through Christ is secure—His victory has become your victory! Living in the power of the Holy Spirit, you are an overcomer.

When the Holy Spirit dwells in you—the same Spirit that raised Jesus from the dead—you experience not only resurrection power, but redemption power. You discover that you are no longer bound by the darkness because you are now illuminated from within by heavenly light. You discover that you are no longer enslaved to destructive habits because you have been set free from the power of sin. You discover that you are no longer limited to what you can do in your own power because now you have Christ's power to overcome death inside you.

Long before the Day of Pentecost, God's people were told to expect these discoveries: "Then your light will break forth like the dawn, and your healing will quickly appear; then your righteousness will go before you, and the glory of the LORD will be your rear guard" (Isaiah 58:8). The prophet Isaiah spoke these words of God's truth to His people while they were in captivity. The Israelites were defeated spiritually, emotionally, psychologically, financially, and physically. At this time, God's people were begging and pleading for even the smallest spark of hope, likely wondering if they would ever experience victory of any kind again.

But then came the word of the Lord.

Still today, there is nothing more powerful than "Thus saith the Lord!"

This prophetic word from Isaiah still applies to us today, even as we live in its fulfillment as overcomers in the power of the Holy Spirit. This word of the Lord brings heaven to earth and enables you to overcome your hell. This word brings wisdom and truth to dispel and defeat the diabolically fabricated lies of the enemy in your life.

If you're struggling with the challenges of life, the temptations of the enemy, or the residual baggage of your past, then the word of the Lord reminds you that you already have the victory you need: "But thanks be to God! He gives us the victory through our Lord

Jesus Christ" (1 Corinthians 15:57). Owning the hope of your salvation means that you already know what comes next. No matter what you might be experiencing right now, you have the same Spirit within you that won the victory over death through the resurrection of Jesus. Your victory is in the present tense.

Victory is not coming.

Victory is not on the way.

Victory is not a futuristic concept to be embraced upon its arrival.

Victory is not the conditional result of some future battle.

Your victory has already been secured.

Your victory has already been given.

Your victory has already been implemented.

In Christ, with Christ, for Christ, you have victory!

SCRIPTURE

For everyone who has been born of God overcomes the world. And this is the victory that has overcome the world—our faith. Who is it that overcomes the world except the one who believes that Jesus is the Son of God?

—1 John 5:4–5 ESV

—————————— **PRAYER** ——————————

Dear Jesus, Your victory over sin and death means that my salvation is secure! Your victory on the cross has now become my victory. Through the power of Your Spirit in me, I can overcome any adversity I may face today. Amen.

Day 27

Stop praying *for* victory and start praying *from* victory! Experiencing the holy fire of God's Spirit, you can know that your victory has been won.

When you're facing the push-pull of life's challenges, victory might seem elusive, a future triumph you will experience someday. But the reality is that you have victory right now, even in the process of overcoming. You received victory when God filled you with the gift of the Holy Spirit, which means your victory is happening right now!

So you can stop praying for victory. You can quit asking others to pray for your victory. You can end your fasting in the hope that victory will come. No longer do you need to praise and worship so that you can know victory. You will not be victorious one day—*you are victorious today!* The moment you are born again, you are automatically, permanently, and perfectly victorious. Victory is already yours.

Don't pray for victory—pray *from* victory.

Don't praise for victory—praise *from* victory.

Don't fast for victory—fast *from* victory.

Accept the spiritual reality that you are victorious. Wherever you look, you will see victory. "For the LORD your God is the one who goes with you to fight for you against your enemies to give you victory" (Deuteronomy 20:4). Wherever you go, you will experience victory. "For everyone born of God overcomes the world. This is the victory that has overcome the world, even our faith" (1 John 5:4).

Whether you look right or left, go east or west, or jump up and down, you will find victory. Victory means you have no other choice but to overcome. To overcome is to defeat, to conquer, to triumph, to win. When you are filled with the Holy Spirit, you have no other choice but to overcome.

Abraham overcame his lies.

Joseph overcame the pit and the betrayal of his brothers.

Moses overcame Pharaoh, his temper, and his past.

Joshua overcame Jericho, the disobedience of his troops, and his fear of being alone.

David overcame Saul's spear, a bear, a lion, a giant, and his own moral turpitude.

Esther overcame the haters.

Daniel overcame the lions.

Job overcame the loss of everything.
Peter overcame the cursing of his blessing.
Paul overcame the shipwreck and the snakebite.
And Jesus—Jesus overcame everything!
His victory is your victory.
You are not a victim.
You are not the devil's punching bag.
You are not cursed, condemned, or criticized.
You are a new creature, a co-heir with Christ, God's beloved child!

SCRIPTURE

Behold, I have given you authority to tread on serpents and scorpions, and over all the power of the enemy, and nothing shall hurt you.

—Luke 10:19 ESV

PRAYER

Dear Lord, I will no longer look ahead and wait for victory—because You have already given me Your victory over darkness, death, and defeat! As I rely on the power of Your Holy Spirit today, remind me that I am an overcomer. Amen.

When you are
FILLED
with the Holy Spirit,
you have no other
choice but to
OVERCOME.

Day 28

If trials and temptations obscure your vision, you must look with the eyes of your heart in order to see your victory. When viewed with spiritual sight, your challenges reveal your victory in Christ!

Experiencing the hope of a victory you already have can be difficult to embrace at times. You know you already have the victory, but you struggle to own it by faith when it is not yet manifest visibly. That's when you must see with the eyes of your heart and not merely the eyes in your head. Paul told the believers at Ephesus, "I pray that the eyes of your heart may be enlightened in order that you may know the hope to which he has called you, the riches of his glorious inheritance in his holy people" (Ephesians 1:18).

Why does Paul pray this? So that they will know the hope to which God has called them and experience the riches of God's glorious inheritance. Seeing with the eyes of your heart yields spiritual enlightenment. This allows the Spirit within you to look beyond what the eyes in your body can envision.

When you look with the eyes of your heart, you can see the invisible reality of victory because of the power of the Spirit within you. What you look upon may resemble defeat temporarily. What attracts your attention may appear to be dormant, stagnant, or inactive. What disrupts your life when it blindsides you may seem to knock you down. But no matter what you experience, when you look with the eyes of your heart, you will still see victory.

When you look at your children and your children's children, you will see victory.

When you look at your marriage, you will see victory.

When you look at your health report, you will see victory.

When you look at your financial accounts, you will see victory.

When you look at your résumé, you will see victory.

When you look at your *now*, you will see victory.

When you look at your *next*, you will see victory.

From this moment on, you will pray from victory.

From this moment on, you will praise from victory.

From this moment on, you will worship from victory.

You are stepping into not just a season, but a *lifetime* of victory.

Victory defines you and your family and your loved ones as you pursue righteousness in the name of Jesus. Victory describes who you are as a new creature in Christ, God's still-in-progress masterpiece, and more than a conqueror. Victory determines how you measure your steps each day as you follow the guiding voice of the Spirit within you.

You will live in and with the victory of salvation all the days of your life!

SCRIPTURE

Jesus looked at them and said, "With man this is impossible, but not with God; all things are possible with God."

—Mark 10:27

PRAYER

Dear God, strengthen my faith so that when I cannot see victory in the midst of my circumstances, I can look with the eyes of my heart and know the truth of Your triumph. Relying on the power of Your Spirit, I want to live victoriously in every area of my life! Amen.

Day 29

Keep your connection to the power of the Holy Spirit by focusing on the foundation for your faith—salvation through Christ Jesus alone!

Sometimes we get so caught up in our lives, in our families and our careers, in our personal struggles and private battles, that we overlook the unshakable foundation of our faith. Even churches lose sight of this most important aspect: making sure that every member of the flock has a personal, intimate relationship with the good Shepherd, Jesus Christ. We often get so bogged down in the minutia of life and peripheral issues of human existence that we neglect the most important message that can come out of any believer's mouth, any church's pulpit, any event's podium.

Too often, we're focused on what is nonessential instead of what is essential. We get caught up in twelve steps to feeling good, ten steps to looking better, seven steps for financial prosperity, five steps for better relationships, and three steps for eating all you want without counting calories. We get excited about mastery before we know the Master.

If you want to maintain your connection to your spiritual power source, then you must focus on what is essential, foundational, and fundamental: You have the victory of salvation that only comes from Christ. "Salvation is found in no one else, for there is no other name under heaven given to mankind by which we must be saved" (Acts 4:12).

There is no greater joy than the joy of salvation.

There is no greater peace than the peace of salvation.

There is no greater promise than the promise of salvation.

The joy we have as believers doesn't come from the world, which means the world cannot take it away. The Spirit in us—the same Spirit that hovered and covered the world before it was formed, the same Spirit that raised Jesus from the dead, the same Spirit that descended on 120 believers at Pentecost—that Spirit is in us. The world didn't give us that Spirit, and the world can never take that Spirit away from us. Jesus won the victory and set us free.

When you are saved, you walk a little differently.

When you are saved, you talk differently.

When you are saved, you give differently.

When you are saved, you love differently.
When you are saved, you praise differently.
When you are saved, you pray differently.
When you are saved, you live differently.

When you are saved, you have a glorious hope because of the victory of your salvation. Not wishful thinking. Not castles in the air. Not daydreams that fade away. A living, glorious, victorious hope!

SCRIPTURE

Therefore, since we have been justified through faith, we have peace with God through our Lord Jesus Christ, through whom we have gained access by faith into this grace in which we now stand. And we boast in the hope of the glory of God.

—Romans 5:1–2

PRAYER

Jesus, I am so grateful that salvation is found in You and You alone! The joy of my salvation can never be taken away—not by the world, not by circumstances, not by my feelings. Through the power of Your Spirit in me, I can boast in the hope of Your glory. Amen.

Day 30

Jesus is in a place all by Himself—the Incarnation, Immanuel, God with us in human form. When you have His Spirit within you, others see God's power shining through!

Whrough you are saved, you want to elevate Jesus above everything and everyone else. You want everyone in the world to know who He is and how much He loves them—enough to die for them. You want them to see His Spirit within you and the transformative impact He has had on your life. You want everyone around you to recognize that Jesus is unlike anyone they have ever met or will ever meet.

We want others to see the light of Christ shining in us just as some of the disciples witnessed a supernatural transformation in their Master: "And as he was praying, the appearance of his face was transformed, and his clothes became dazzling white. Suddenly, two men, Moses and Elijah, appeared and began talking with Jesus. They were glorious to see. And they were speaking about his exodus from this world, which was about to be fulfilled in Jerusalem" (Luke 9:29–31 NLT).

Peter, James, and John had gone with Jesus up to a mountain in order to pray together, but while praying, their Master's face was transformed—glowing, radiating, and beaming. His clothes were not just white, but *dazzling* white. Then two of the greatest prophets in Jewish history, Moses and Elijah, appeared and began talking to Jesus about His imminent departure.

This is not merely a surreal scene—it was *glorious* to see.

Why? Because it reflects God's glory in visible, dramatic, neon-bright fashion. This is heaven touching earth. This is Jesus on the red carpet. This is the Messiah with the spotlight of heaven shining on Him.

Then, suddenly, He's not alone—we've got guest stars!

Symbolically speaking, Moses represents the Jewish Law, the old system for relating to God, and Elijah represents Jewish prophecy, which foretold the new way—the way embodied in their midst in the form of Jesus Christ, the promised Messiah, the Son of God. While surprising, Jesus next to Moses and Elijah reveals less of a contrast and more of a fulfillment. Because the

Transfiguration, as this event is called, brings complete clarity to any and all questions left over in the Old Covenant of following the Law.

The Transfiguration reveals the moment when heaven proclaimed to the world that Jesus is not equal to Moses or to Elijah or to any of the prophets or any of the previous kings or any of the leaders or any other person in human history.

Jesus is in a place all by Himself.

Jesus is above Moses.

Jesus is above Elijah.

Jesus is God with skin.

Jesus is the Incarnation, Immanuel, God with us in human form.

Jesus is your Savior, who lived, died, was buried, and rose again!

 **SCRIPTURE**

Therefore God exalted him to the highest place and gave him the name that is above every name, that at the name of Jesus every knee should bow, in heaven and on earth and under the earth, and every tongue acknowledge that Jesus Christ is Lord, to the glory of God the Father.

—Philippians 2:9–11

PRAYER

Lord Jesus, I give You praise, honor, and glory! You did what no one else could ever do and saved me from my sins. You gave me the power of Your Spirit within me— the same Spirit that raised You from the dead. Amen.

Day 31

If you want the same Spirit that raised Jesus from the dead to transform you into His likeness, then elevate Christ in all areas of your life. When you lift Him up, He will lift you up!

If you want to live in the power of the Holy Spirit, you must elevate Jesus—because no one is His equal. He's not a good leader with some divine commandments to share, like Moses. He's not a prophet sent to speak on behalf of God regarding future events. He's not a great rabbi sent to teach the Torah. He's not a social activist who tried to overthrow the Roman occupation and restore Israel to prominence as a nation.

Jesus is the living Son of God, who saves us from all our sins!

We must stop placing Jesus on the same stage with anyone else, with cultural, political, religious, historical influencers and leaders both past and present. Jesus is not their equal. Jesus is above every king, queen, president, actor, singer, celebrity, artist, writer, and social media influencer. Jesus is above every preacher, pastor, and ministry leader.

Why is Jesus incomparably above everyone else? Simply put, because "there is salvation in no one else! God has given no other name under heaven by which we must be saved" (Acts 4:12 NLT). There is no one like Jesus.

So stop placing Jesus on equal footing or on the same stage with the other important influencers in your life. Stop acting like your faith is just a lifestyle fad you're trying out to see if it works. Stop letting your faith run hot or cold depending on your circumstances. Stop living like you are anyone other than a child of the King, a co-heir with Christ, an overcomer who can do all things—not just some things, or even hard things, but *all* things—through Christ, who strengthens you!

If you want the same Spirit in you to transform you into the likeness of Jesus, keep your eyes fixed on Him. When you lift Him up, He will lift you up. Your elevation is directly proportional to His exaltation. "Seek the Kingdom of God above all else, and live righteously, and he will give you everything you need" (Matthew 6:33 NLT).

Jesus is not equal to your family.

Jesus is not equal to your career.

Jesus is not equal to your bank account.

Jesus is not equal to your social media presence.

Jesus is not even equal to your ministry or your calling.

Jesus is not equal to Moses or Elijah, to the Law or the prophets.

Jesus is the fulfillment of these, and therefore, above everything and everyone else!

Only Jesus is Lord.

Only Jesus is Savior.

Only Jesus is worthy of your praise!

Only Jesus is worthy of your honor!

Only Jesus is worthy of your worship!

Only Jesus.

 **SCRIPTURE**

By his divine power, God has given us everything we need for living a godly life. We have received all of this by coming to know him, the one who called us to himself by means of his marvelous glory and excellence.

—2 Peter 1:3 NLT

―――――――――― **PRAYER** ――――――――――

Dear Jesus, forgive me for the times when I have not elevated You above all others in my life. No one is equal to You, and no one could do all that You have done in my life. Thank You for Your love and mercy, for Your power and grace. Only You are worthy of all honor, praise, and glory! Amen.

If you want to

LIVE

in the power
of the Holy Spirit,
you must elevate
Jesus—because

NO ONE

is His equal.

Day 32

No matter how broken we are, the same Spirit
that raised Jesus from the dead brings healing.
God not only saves us—He also heals us!

We live in a broken world filled with broken
people. Broken families, broken children,
broken generations. Nations are broken,
cities are broken, communities are broken. We are broken physically, mentally, spiritually, relationally, and financially. When we stop and look around us, we witness a world on life support, sick and gasping for breath, wounded and bleeding out.

Broken by sin, we're wounded by words, as well as sickened by silence. We carry secrets that manifest in our bodies as the weight of our burdens crushes our minds, hearts, and spirits. Wounded people bleed on others and injure them as well, often those they love the most. Broken people break people, hurting people hurt people, and traumatized people traumatize people.

But here is God's promise, the word of the Lord given to His people thousands of years ago and still just as timeless and relevant today: "Salvation will come like the dawn, and your wounds will quickly heal. Your godliness will lead you forward, and the glory of the LORD will protect you from behind" (Isaiah 58:8 NLT). God promised that salvation comes like the dawn because He is our God who saves. But He is also our God who heals!

Healing is such an essential aspect of who God is, and we see this reflected in one of the names by which He is known. After God liberated the Israelites from Egyptian captivity, they spent three days in the desert and desperately needed water. When they finally found a river, the water was contaminated and undrinkable. So God instructed them to put a piece of wood in the water, which they did, and He purified the water.

Following this incident, they received the word of the Lord: "If you listen carefully to the LORD your God and do what is right in his eyes, if you pay attention to his commands and keep all his decrees, I will not bring on you any of the diseases I brought on the Egyptians, for I am the LORD, who heals you" (Exodus 15:26).

The original Hebrew for this last descriptor is *Jehovah Rapha*, "the LORD who heals you."

God is the Great I AM—if He was the Lord who heals then, then He is the Lord who heals now. If He healed the Israelites then, then He will heal you now! Your wounds will quickly heal (Isaiah 58:8 NLT) because healing is God's promise to His children. If God did it before, He will do it again!

You have the resurrection power of the Holy Spirit— Jehovah Rapha—in you!

SCRIPTURE

[The LORD] forgives all your sins and heals all your diseases.

—Psalm 103:3

PRAYER

Jehovah Rapha, thank You for being the God who heals me! You know the broken places inside my heart, as well as all that's broken around me. I trust You for complete healing, Lord, inside and out, because nothing is impossible for You. Amen.

Day 33

Don't overlook the healing power available to you through the power of the Holy Spirit. It only takes one touch!

Jesus healed many people throughout His ministry on earth, but one stands out because it illustrates the power of faith in action. Rather than waiting on God's healing touch to come to her, one desperate woman decided to find healing by touching the Lord. After suffering with constant bleeding for twelve years, this woman was at the end of her rope.

She had spent all her money on doctors, who not only failed to help her condition, but actually made it worse. Hearing about Jesus, this woman waded through the crowd, came up behind Him, and touched His garment, thinking to herself, "If I can just touch his robe, I will be healed" (Mark 5:28 NLT). This desperate woman saw an opportunity—her only remaining option—and stepped out in faith and took it.

There are many things this woman did not have. She had lost all her resources, funding, and hope in the medical professionals of her day. She had no money, no resources, no health insurance, no Social Security, no options remaining except one—she had faith! She believed, "If I touch Him, I will be healed!"

Instead of focusing on what she didn't have, she moved forward with what she did have. She had faith that Jesus, the Messiah, the Man moving through the crowd only a few feet away from her, had the power to heal her. There was no time to try to stop Him and explain all she had been through. There was no opportunity to describe the ordeal of suffering she had endured for twelve long years. But there was an opportunity for her to touch Jesus, to reach out and graze her fingertips along the hem of His robe as He passed by. She only needed one touch!

How often do we become so fixated on what we don't have that we lose sight of all we have by faith?

How often do we so obsess about what we lack that we overlook our greatest gift?

How often do we whine about what we need rather than praise God for what we have?

This woman's faith reminds us that it's not about what you're missing—it's about what you have! We fall into the trap of conditional thinking—"If only I had more money, if only I knew the right specialists, if only

I lived somewhere else, if only . . ." No, this woman had nothing except the one thing that matters most—faith in Jehovah Rapha!

Stop focusing on what's missing—and start shouting about what you have.

You have the power of the Holy Spirit in you!

The same Spirit that raised Jesus from the dead!

SCRIPTURE

Then the frightened woman, trembling at the realization of what had happened to her, came and fell to her knees in front of him and told him what she had done. And he said to her, "Daughter, your faith has made you well. Go in peace. Your suffering is over."

—Mark 5:33–34 NLT

PRAYER

Thank You, Lord, for the power of Your healing touch in my life. When I start to focus on what I lack, remind me of what I have. When I fail to experience healing when I want or the way I want, give me patience to trust You for all my needs. Amen.

Day 34

Don't wait on God to touch you with healing when you can reach out to Him. You are no longer waiting for a miracle—there's a miracle waiting for you!

On your journey of faith, you will experience dark valleys that require you to keep walking by faith. But not only can God reach you when you're enduring pain—when you're enduring pain, you can reach Him! This long-suffering woman who had been hemorrhaging for twelve years broke through the crowd and reached out in faith to touch the robe of her only hope for healing—Jesus (Mark 5:25–34).

She reminds us that we don't have to be perfect to receive God's healing, to experience His love. God uses imperfect people to advance His perfect agenda.

God uses broken people who dare to touch Him to heal a broken world! Our Christian faith is less about promoting the perfect and more about blessing the broken. Because God never rejects the broken: "The sacrifice you desire is a broken spirit. You will not reject a broken and repentant heart, O God" (Psalm 51:17 NLT).

Coming up behind Jesus, this woman reached out to touch His robe while He wasn't even looking or seeming to notice. In fact, He was en route to heal Jairus's daughter, the next generation, when this woman touched Him for her own healing. God did not touch her—she touched God!

She understood that if she entered into His presence, then the power would be released. She didn't have to touch His hand or His hair, His elbow or His ankle. She just needed to touch the robe He was wearing. She had faith that was at least the size of a mustard seed because she believed, "If I can just touch His robe, I'll be healed!"

It's time we relied on the power of God's Spirit within us and reached out to touch God instead of sitting around waiting on Him to touch us. It's time to be so zealous about our belief that we will touch God even when we're not sure He's looking our way! It's time to be so radical and so provocative that we will cause God to look our way!

It takes radical, circumstance-shattering, life-altering, heaven-exciting, hell-upsetting faith to break through failure, rejection, shame, hurt, and brokenness and touch Jesus! For "in your presence there is fullness of joy" (Psalm 16:11 ESV). And it only takes one touch!

It's time to stand out from the crowd and go touch Jesus.

Touch Him with your fears, your doubts, your brokenness.

Touch Him with your pain, your paralysis, your pandemic.

Touch Him with your worries, your wonders, your weaknesses.

Touch Him with your trials, your temptations, your triumphs.

Stop waiting for a miracle—because there's a miracle waiting for you!

Rise up, reach up, raise your hands, and *touch the power of Jesus!*

─────────── **SCRIPTURE** ───────────

Heal me, LORD, and I will be healed; save me and I will be saved, for you are the one I praise.

—Jeremiah 17:14

---------------- **PRAYER** ----------------

Dear God, I reach out to You for the healing power available through Your Holy Spirit in me. Strengthen my faith so that I may trust You even when I cannot see a way forward. Your power and presence provide my comfort and confidence. Amen.

God uses

IMPERFECT PEOPLE

to advance His

PERFECT AGENDA.

Day 35

Filled with the power of the Holy Spirit, you will attract other people's attention. They will notice a divine difference in everything about you!

When we are filled by the same Spirit that descended at Pentecost, we cannot keep silent, because the message of the Gospel is a universal language. In computer science, a universal language is command code that is understandable and transferable to all operating systems. Universal programming language can express any algorithm or computational function in ways accessible to virtually any and all other computer systems' languages.

When you are filled by the Holy Spirit, your life is lived in translation! You are an advertisement for all that God is doing in your life through the power of the Spirit. Others will notice a divine difference in your life and will hear the message you're speaking—regardless of the earthly sounds you utter! They will be drawn to you even as you point them to God.

Of course, some people will not choose to listen or to hear with spiritual ears open to the Gospel. The heavenly language spoken through the Holy Spirit will not make sense to them, because it defies the logic of their senses. "For the message of the cross is foolishness to those who are perishing, but to us who are being saved it is the power of God" (1 Corinthians 1:18). Their hearts will be resistant and closed to the invitation extended to them by the language of the Holy Spirit.

These people will respond like others did that day at Pentecost: "But others in the crowd ridiculed them, saying, 'They're just drunk, that's all!'" (Acts 2:13 NLT). Rather than marveling at the ability to hear the message in their native language, some apparently heard only gibberish and indecipherable sounds. The only explanation they could come up with, based on earthly, mortal logic, was that the believers must have been sloshed, wasted, buzzed, hammered, plastered, inebriated, and intoxicated! They assumed these Spirit-filled believers must have been drunk with wine.

When you live in the power of the same Spirit, others may mistakenly assume the worst about you. They will at times ridicule you, unfollow you, troll you, and mock you. They may say that you must be drunk or high, that you must be out of your mind, that you've lost all common sense or any touch with reality. They will look for scientific explanations or medical rationales rather than acknowledge the power of the Holy Spirit at work in your life. But you know the truth—you are directly in touch with the ultimate reality of the cross of Jesus Christ!

The same Spirit that raised Him from the dead now dwells in you!

SCRIPTURE

Now, Lord, consider their threats and enable your servants to speak your word with great boldness. Stretch out your hand to heal and perform signs and wonders through the name of your holy servant Jesus.

—Acts 4:29–30

PRAYER

Dear God, I pray that the people around me will notice a difference in my life and recognize the healing that has taken place so I can tell them of Your power. Today, I acknowledge You—and You alone—as the Source of the transformation taking place in me. Amen.

Day 36

Your anointing in the Holy Spirit is the foundation for your transformation into the likeness of Christ. You are not just occupying space—you are a temple of the same Spirit that raised Jesus from the dead!

If you want to serve as a spiritual, countercultural alternative to the heartbreaking narrative of this broken world, then accept your anointing to speak in the language of the Word Made Flesh, Jesus Christ! In our world today, with so many different people confused and uncertain, so many identifying with so many descriptors, so many adjectives, so many pronouns, so many pluralities, you can respond in a way that will provoke demons to flee. You are anointed to proclaim the Good News and set captives free. You are anointed to overcome. You are anointed to heal. You are anointed to lead.

Our world is full of other spirits right now—like these, identified in Scripture:

The spirit of divination (Acts 16:16–18).

The spirit of jealousy (Galatians 5:20).

The spirit of deception/lying (Revelation 12:10).

The spirit of perversion (2 Peter 2:14).

The spirit of heaviness (Isaiah 61:3).

The spirit of fear (2 Timothy 1:7).

The spirit of death (1 Corinthians 15:26).

The spirit of the antichrist (1 John 2:18–19).

But there's only one *Holy Spirit*—the same Spirit that was hovering when the earth was still formless and empty (Genesis 1:1–2) . . .

The same Spirit that enabled Joshua to survive the desert, cross over the Jordan, shout down the walls of Jericho, and step into the Promised Land (Numbers 27:18) . . .

The same Spirit that came upon a shepherd boy, enabling him to defeat the giant called Goliath, to conquer the city of Jerusalem, and to bring back the Ark of the Covenant (1 Samuel 16:13) . . .

If you want to live out of your anointing, if you want order instead of chaos, if you want life instead of death, if you want springs of living water instead of drought, if you want to cross over your Jordan and shout down the obstacles in front of you and step into the place God has for you, if you want to bring down the giant looming in your way, then the Holy Spirit is essential!

If you want to possess your destiny, reflect God's glory, and experience the fullness of life Jesus came to bring, then your anointing in the Holy Spirit is the foundation—the foundation for your transformation into Christ's likeness! "Do you not know that you are God's temple and that God's Spirit dwells in you?" (1 Corinthians 3:16 ESV).

You are not just a human being—you are a spiritual being.

You do not only occupy space—you house divinity.

You are not just another person—you are a temple of the Holy Spirit!

You are anointed for more!

SCRIPTURE

And it is God who establishes us with you in Christ, and has anointed us, and who has also put his seal on us and given us his Spirit in our hearts as a guarantee.

—2 Corinthians 1:21–22 ESV

—————————— **PRAYER** ——————————

Dear Lord, thank You for the gift of my anointing through the Holy Spirit. Today, I pray that I would shine Your divine light into the darkness of the lives of those who do not know You. I am so grateful to be a temple of Your Spirit. Amen.

You are anointed
TO OVERCOME.
You are anointed
TO HEAL.
You are anointed
TO LEAD.

Day 37

Your anointing in and through the Holy Spirit continues from season to season. As you advance in your anointing, others cannot help but notice the power of God in your life.

When you receive the Holy Spirit, you are anointed for more! You are anointed for your assignment, for your acceptance, and for your advancement. Once David was king over Israel, he still had lessons to learn and growth to experience, particularly regarding how he used his power and the price of yielding to temptation (2 Samuel 5:3). This was his advanced anointing. He had accepted his assignment when Samuel, instructed by God, anointed David as the next king. He then fulfilled his assignment by accepting the throne when King Saul died. But David continued to advance in his anointing and to grow in his faith.

Through the finished work of Jesus Christ on the cross, you are also anointed to advance into all that the Lord has for you. When you abide in the Holy Spirit, your anointing explodes with spiritual dynamite in ways that not only change you, but also change the world around you. You are anointed when the grace, gift, and glory of God inside you come together, enabling you to experience the abundant power of heaven come to earth.

What do you do once you move into your advanced anointing?

Following the example of Jesus, you go about doing good and healing the oppressed: "How God anointed Jesus of Nazareth with the Holy Spirit and with power. He went about doing good and healing all who were oppressed by the devil, for God was with him" (Acts 10:38 ESV). You overcome evil and heal the sick: "And they cast out many demons and anointed with oil many who were sick and healed them" (Mark 6:13 ESV). You pray and anoint others: "Is anyone among you sick? Let him call for the elders of the church, and let them pray over him, anointing him with oil in the name of the Lord" (James 5:14 ESV).

From Genesis to Revelation and still today, we discover that anointed people do what others will not do. Anointed people do what others *cannot* do. When you abide in the power of the Spirit and live out your anointing, you speak the language of grace. Your speech, your attitude, and your actions communicate Jesus in ways that cause others to notice.

Anointed people do not whine—they worship.

Anointed people do not focus on the darkness—they turn on the light.

Anointed people do not make excuses—they make history.

Like David, like Peter and the believers at Pentecost, you are anointed by the Spirit of God. You live today because you have a God-appointed, God-orchestrated, God-ordained assignment. You are uniquely qualified for the anointing you have through the Holy Spirit!

--- **SCRIPTURE** ---

You have loved righteousness and hated wickedness; therefore God, your God, has anointed you with the oil of gladness beyond your companions.

—Hebrews 1:9 ESV

PRAYER

Dear God, I pray that You would continue to reveal all that You have anointed me to experience and accomplish in my life. Open my eyes, Lord, to the advanced anointing that awaits me. Empower me through Your Spirit to fulfill my divine destiny. Amen.

Day 38

As you advance in your anointing, you will encounter Spirit-filled partners who will help you grow and assist in fulfilling your divine destiny. You can trust God to show you whom you can trust!

A s you abide and grow in the same Spirit, you will discover the power of partnerships with others willing to praise with you, to pray with you, and to persevere with you. Jesus told us that we experience His presence in our midst and amplify our prayers to heaven when we gather with others: "Again, I give you an eternal truth: If two of you agree to ask God for something in a symphony of prayer, my heavenly Father will do it for you. For wherever two or three come together in honor of my name, I am right there with them!" (Matthew 18:19–20 TPT).

There comes a season as you advance in your anointing when God will remove dream killers and replace them with dream weavers. When you are experiencing spiritual growing pains, one of the most important prayers you can make is asking God to remove the wrong people from your life and to bring the right people into your life. Trust that God will surround you with people who will help you fulfill your divine destiny!

Keep in mind, however, that not everyone can accept your anointing.

Some people can handle your struggle, but not your success.

Some people can be with you when you're broken and busted, but they can't handle you when you're blessed and favored.

Because some people want you to depend on them in perpetuity, they get high off your dependency because of your validation of them and their value. Rather than relying on the Holy Spirit, rather than living from the center of their identity in Christ, they look to you, to other people, for some semblance of an identity. That's why you need people who are with you both when you're up and when you're down. When you're wounded and when you're healed. When you accept your anointing and when you advance in your anointing.

When considering when and whom to trust, first ask yourself two other questions: Do you trust God for everything? and, Can God trust you with anything? Once you can affirmatively and confidently answer these two questions, then you are ready to ask, "Whom can I trust?"

As you grow in the Spirit, you will also grow in wisdom and discernment. You will be more attuned to the voice of God, and therefore, you will become a better spiritual listener. You will know you cannot grow into the fullness of all God has for you without other people, without key partnerships and a Spirit-filled community of believers. You will trust that God will show you whom you can trust for the next season of your anointing.

———————— **SCRIPTURE** ————————

Be completely humble and gentle; be patient, bearing with one another in love. Make every effort to keep the unity of the Spirit through the bond of peace.

—Ephesians 4:2–3

PRAYER

Lord, thank You for sending people into my life who support, challenge, and encourage me in my relationship with You. Give me discernment about who should not be in my life and who should be my spiritual partners for this current season of anointing. Amen.

Day 39

God's power fertilizes the soil of your mistakes, your flaws, and your weaknesses to produce what you cannot grow on your own—the fruit of His Spirit!

As you grow in the Spirit and advance in your anointing, your life will bear spiritual fruit. In order to live fruitfully, however, you must abide in Christ—because no one can bear fruit by themselves or by their own power. Just as a branch cut off from its tree trunk cannot produce fruit and will eventually die, you do not have the power to grow spiritual fruit in your own ability. Left to your own attempts and efforts, you will fail.

When we remain in Jesus, though, and He remains in us through the indwelling of the Holy Spirit, we bear much fruit. When we abide in Christ and nourish our faith with His words, God's truth, we grow in maturity and produce divine fruit—love, joy, peace, patience, kindness, goodness, faithfulness, gentleness, and self-control. These variations are all the same fruit of the Spirit.

When you live in your anointing and obey God into the next season of your anointing, your fruit ripens. Your roots grow deeper in the soil of faith. Your nourishment comes from your Life-Source, the Holy Spirit. Divine love blossoms in your thoughts, your words, your attitudes and actions.

You don't rely on circumstances, money, or other people to make you happy, because you have the joy of heaven growing inside you.

You don't get anxious and depressed by overwhelming demands and the noise of a chaotic world consuming you, because you have peace that passes understanding.

You don't have to fight to be first, step on the backs of others to advance, or exploit opportunities for advancement, because you have faith-fueled patience to trust God's timing.

You don't have to compete, compare, envy, and covet others—on social media, in your neighborhood, at church—because divine compassion blooms from God's kindness in you.

You don't have to work harder to pursue perfection or be a better person, because your goodness comes from the ultimate Source—God's goodness and generosity.

You don't have to force yourself to participate in church, tithe and make offerings, praise and worship, confess and forgive, because your faithfulness comes from the Holy Spirit in you.

You don't have to soften your strength or dial down your divine anointing, because gentleness characterizes everything you say and do.

You don't beat yourself up when you stumble or yield to temptation, because your sins have been forgiven and the Holy Spirit is your strength.

This is the fruit of the Spirit growing in you!

 **SCRIPTURE**

I am the vine; you are the branches. If you remain in me and I in you, you will bear much fruit; apart from me you can do nothing.

—John 15:5

 **PRAYER**

Dear Jesus, help me to abide in You as I grow in my dependence on Your Holy Spirit. Let all areas of my life produce the fruit of the Spirit so that others can experience Your love, grace, and goodness. Amen.

As you grow
in the Spirit and
ADVANCE
in your anointing,
your life will bear
SPIRITUAL FRUIT.

Day 40

Get ready for the anointing of fresh oil, the power
of holy fire, and the blessing of new wine in your
life. The same Spirit that raised Jesus from the
dead dwells in you!

You are stepping into a season of fresh oil, holy
fire, and new wine in order to experience the
Spirit-filled life at the next level! You are advancing in your anointing, growing stronger in the power of
the Spirit, and overflowing with blessings. How is this
possible? Because . . .

The same Spirit that raised Jesus from the dead
dwells in you.

The same Spirit that anointed David with fresh oil
anoints you.

The same Spirit that ignited believers at Pentecost
burns in you.

The same Spirit that has shown favor to God's followers now blesses you.

You are receiving fresh oil, holy fire, and new wine to get back everything that was lost. Everything that was stolen, corrupted, and held back—*everything*. You're getting back all you've lost—and more!

You're getting your joy back.

You're getting your peace back.

You're getting your family back.

You're getting your health back.

God wants to anoint you for what's next with fresh oil.

God wants to empower you for what's next with holy fire.

God wants to bless you for what's next with new wine.

The source for your fresh oil, holy fire, and new wine?

The same Spirit that raised Christ from the dead!

There's no better declaration of what you can expect next than what Paul wrote to the church at Philippi. "I want to know Christ and experience the mighty power that raised him from the dead" (Philippians 3:10 NLT). Knowing Jesus allows you to access the same power source that defeated death and restored life. There's no mistake—this Spirit is one and the same as the One who is in you.

The same Spirit that brought Jesus out of the tomb is more than powerful enough to take you out of the worst season and into the best season, from death to life. The same Spirit of the Lord is upon you in power. So get ready for even more transformation!

To every Joseph with a dream, you're not in the pit anymore.

To every Moses with a past, you're not in Egypt anymore.

To every Joshua with a milk-and-honey vision, you're not in the desert anymore.

To every Ruth and Naomi, you're not in Moab anymore.

To every Shadrach, Meshach, and Abednego, you're not in the furnace anymore.

To every Peter and John, Paul and Silas, you're not in prison anymore.

To every Lazarus buried and left for dead, you're not in the tomb anymore.

No matter where you are or what you're facing, you have the same Spirit.

Through the resurrection power of the same Spirit, get ready to experience fresh oil, holy fire, and new wine!

--- **SCRIPTURE** ---

The Spirit of God, who raised Jesus from the dead, lives in you. And just as God raised Christ Jesus from the dead, he will give life to your mortal bodies by this same Spirit living within you.

—Romans 8:11 NLT

 **PRAYER**

Holy Spirit, thank You for dwelling in me. May I continue to rely on You more and more, to advance in my anointing and to produce Your fruit. Amen.

SAMUEL RODRIGUEZ is president of the National Hispanic Christian Leadership Conference (NHCLC), the world's largest Hispanic Christian organization, with more than 42,000 U.S. churches and many additional churches spread throughout the Spanish-speaking diaspora.

Rodriguez stands recognized by CNN, Fox News, Univision, and Telemundo as America's most influential Latino/Hispanic faith leader. *Charisma* magazine named him one of the forty leaders who have changed the world. The *Wall Street Journal* named him one of the top-twelve Latino leaders, and he was the only faith leader on that list. He has been named among the "Top 100 Christian Leaders in America" (*Newsmax* 2018) and nominated as one of the "100 Most Influential People in the World" (*Time* 2013). Rodriguez is regularly featured on CNN, Fox News, Univision, PBS, *Christianity Today*, the *New York Times*, the *Wall Street Journal*, and many others.

Rodriguez was the first Latino to deliver the keynote address at the annual Martin Luther King Jr. Commemorative Service at Ebenezer Baptist Church, and he is a recipient of the Martin Luther King Jr. Leadership Award presented by the Congress of Racial Equality.

Rodriguez advised former American presidents Bush, Obama, and Trump, and he frequently consults with Congress regarding advancing immigration and criminal justice reform as well as religious freedom and pro-life initiatives. By the grace of God, the Rev. Samuel Rodriguez is one of the few individuals to have participated in the inauguration ceremonies of two different presidents representing both political parties.

In January 2009, Pastor Sam read from the gospel of Luke for Mr. Obama's inaugural morning service at Saint John's Episcopal Church. On January 20, 2017, at Mr. Trump's inauguration, with more than one billion people watching from around the world, Pastor Sam became the first Latino evangelical to participate in a U.S. presidential inaugural ceremony, reading from Matthew 5 and concluding with "in Jesus' name!" In April 2020, Reverend Rodriguez was appointed to the National Coronavirus Recovery Commission to offer specialized experience and expertise in crisis mitigation and recovery to help national, state, and local leaders guide America through the COVID-19 pandemic.

Rodriguez is the executive producer of two films: *Breakthrough*, the GMA Dove Award winner for Inspirational Film of the Year, with an Academy Award nomination for Best Original Song, and *Flamin' Hot*, in partnership with Franklin Entertainment and 20th Century Fox. He is also co-founder of TBN Salsa, an international Christian-based broadcast television network, and he is the author of *You Are Next*, *Shake Free*, *Be Light*—a number-one *L.A. Times* bestseller—and *From Survive to Thrive*, a number-one Amazon bestseller.

He earned his master's degree from Lehigh University and has received honorary doctorates from Northwest University, William Jessup University, and Baptist University of the Americas.

Rodriguez serves as the senior pastor of New Season Church, one of America's fastest-growing megachurches and number thirteen on "Newsmax's Top 50 Megachurches in America," with campuses in Los Angeles and Sacramento, California, where he resides with his wife, Eva, and their three children.

For more information, please visit:

 PastorSam.com

 RevSamuelRodriguez

 @pastorsamuelrodriguez

X @nhclc